100 YEARS OF FOOTBALL

BY JERRY BRONDFIELD

ILLUSTRATED BY
CHARLES BECK

SBS SCHOLASTIC BOOK SERVICES
New York Toronto London Auckland Sydney

2nd printing.. November 1969

Printed in the U.S.A.

Dedicated to G. Herbert McCracken, a great player under Glenn S. (Pop) Warner at the University of Pittsburgh, an outstanding coach at Allegheny College and Lafayette College, and one of the guiding spirits in the growth of Scholastic Magazines, Inc.; and who in his long and constant devotion to Football and Education has been a true All-America.

—*JB and CB*

A Hundred Shining Autumns

It all started on Nov. 6, 1869—one hundred years ago—in a park in New Brunswick, N. J., where a group of Princeton students and another group from Rutgers, 25 to a side, met in the first formal game of intercollegiate football.

Did we say "formal?" Its formality went only insofar as it was a scheduled event, a challenge issued and a challenge accepted, within a framework of barely rudimentary rules of conduct. What it was, was hardly football as we know it now. But it was the germ of an infection that would soon sweep the nation in rapidly changing form until there would be a sport truly unique anywhere in the world. Because, whereas many countries engage in all manner of games, only the Americans—plus their Canadian cousins—have taken to the rousing, rugged contact sport known as football. Make of this what you will. Football, which has now celebrated its Centennial Anniversary, remains *the* uniquely American game, and throughout the years of its development has fondly and passionately come to be regarded as "The Great Autumnal Madness."

Look back at it . . . Amos Alonzo Stagg, Walter Camp, Pudge Heffelfinger, Walter Eckersall, Fielding H. ("Hurry-Up") Yost, Ted Coy, Jim Thorpe, Chic Harley, Bo McMillin, Bob Zuppke, Red Grange, The Four Horsemen of Notre Dame, Knute Rockne, Ernie Nevers, Bronko Nagurski, Jock Sutherland, Pop Warner, Bernie Bierman, Tom Harmon, Otto Graham, Bobby Dodd, Jimmy Brown, Johnny Unitas, Sam Huff, Bart Starr . . . Names, names, and more names! Stars—coaches—legends—fabled teams and drama-packed games.

No sport, we believe, presents a story so colorful and dynamic. Capturing its highlights in the format we have chosen has been a challenge both to historian and artist, and we hope there isn't a flag on the play.

—Jerry Brondfield
Charles Beck

100 Years of Football

American college boys in the 1800's for years had been playing simple ball-kicking games — crude soccer-style affairs (using a round, canvas-covered rubber bladder) with little organization, strategy, or a standard set of rules. But, after the Civil War, a stirring of competition on the campuses made it inevitable that still another team sport, besides baseball, would surely develop soon. ● ●

American intercollegiate football was born when Princeton accepted a challenge from nearby Rutgers for a formal game on Nov. 6, 1869, in a park at New Brunswick, N.J., with 25 to a side, playing under so-called English Association rules.

Running or throwing the ball was banned, but it could be snatched in mid-air or on first bounce for a free kick. About 200 spectators sat on fences or buckboards on the eventful day. The team which first kicked six field goals would be declared winner. There were no uniforms, but Rutgers wore scarlet turbans. Whether this made any difference or not, the Rutgers boys took this history-maker, 6-4. The teams dined together that night and an exciting idea was in the wind.

By 1870 several Eastern colleges were meeting informally in haphazard kicking games and there was a real need for standard rules if the sport were to catch on. ●

In 1872 Princeton drew up football's first written code: a field 500 by 300 feet; 25 players to a side; goal posts to be 25 feet apart; no tripping or shoving; a time limit for each game instead of by a prescribed number of goals kicked. ● ●

But Harvard boys, experimenting, began running short distances with ball before kicking. No other school would play Harvard that way.

I HEAR THOSE HARVARD BLOKES ARE RUNNING WITH THE BALL, TOO. LET'S CHALLENGE THEM!

Meanwhile, at McGill in Montreal, there was a modified form of English Rugby, allowing a man to grab ball and, if he didn't drop it or weren't knocked down, race all the way to the goal for a "touchdown." Canadian football now had an exciting difference, and in 1874 the McGill boys had a novel thought.

WE'VE BEEN CHALLENGED BY McGILL-- LISTEN TO THIS!

Not only did Harvard accept McGill's challenge but agreed to some special considerations Canadians offered.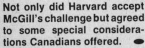

Three games between McGill and Harvard in 1874 were a turning point in football, paving the way for a Rugby-type game featuring "scrummage" (the early spelling). When ball was dead it was placed between massed, opposing teams—

—where players mauled and shoved at each other while trying to kick it into the clear toward foe's goal. Sometimes ball would bounce out of "scrummage" in forward direction. Often it was deflected backwards for a waiting man to control.

But "special consideration" in Harvard-McGill series was players could be "tackled" if they ran the ball: the first hint of "contact" sport.

After McGill, Harvard said it would play the Rugby style and in 1875 Yale accepted a challenge for the nation's first Rugby-type game. Harvard won, 4-0, and all over the East people talked about an exciting new game — a glamorized form of old-style soccer. American football definitely was on a consistent course, if only a group of schools could now agree to operate on certain standards.

Nov. 11, 1876, was a turning point in football. Meeting at Springfield, Mass., Harvard, Yale, Princeton, and Columbia formed the American Intercollegiate Football Association, adopting the Rugby-style game, with 15 players. (Yale held out for 11 to a side and a few years later got its way.) ● ●

Goals were 18 feet wide, with crossbar set 10 feet high. Field was 140 yards by 70. Halves were 45 minutes. ●

GRAB IT AND RUN, JOE!

Scrummage was retained, along with running with the ball and tackling. Goal line could be crossed anywhere.

Games were to be decided by number of touchdowns scored. (But a kicked goal would equal four touchdowns.) Oval-shaped ball replaced round soccer-type.

The first formal uniforms were worn in Penn-Princeton game of 1876: white flannel cricket suits for the Quakers; black shirts and knee pants with orange trim by Tigers. Cleated shoes were still illegal. There was no padding on uniforms.

Making appearance at Yale that year was Walter Camp, destined to be "Father of American Football." ● ● ●

Football in the mid-1870's, however, was still a primitive, non-strategic game. Kicking the ball to advance it was favored over running. A try for a kicked goal (by any player during the constant melee) was favored over an attempt to run for a touchdown. The ball still had to be haphazardly squirted out of the struggling mass of the opposing walls of scrummage forwards after every dead ball or out-of-bounds. These forwards tried to maneuver it to "half tends" slightly behind them who were usually faster and better kickers. ●

IT'S RIDICULOUS FOR STUDENTS TO WASTE TIME LIKE THIS!

In 1878 the primitive game nevertheless drew an amazing crowd of 4000 to see Yale play Princeton on a rented field. The $300 rental fee and the size of the crowd gave rise to the first charges of over-emphasis of student sports activity. ●

By the late '70s the oval-shaped Rugby-type ball had almost displaced the round ball, and kickers were reaching a high degree of accuracy with either foot, by punting, and by a recently discovered scoring technique called the "drop-kick."

But American collegians, perhaps more adventuresome than their Canadian cousins, soon began running more with the ball. It seemed to be more fun than just kicking it. Speed and toughness began to be prime requirements for the game and, for the first time, team captains (there were yet no coaches) began laying down "training rules" for boys who wanted to play. Limits were put on drinking, smoking, and late hours.

Almost simultaneously, Yale and Princeton devised a crude type of interference called "guarding," a simple way to protect runner with a teammate on either side as he ran with ball. (Nobody had yet thought of knocking anyone down.)

CAMP'S RIGHT! ELEVEN MEN WILL GET RID OF A LOT OF CLUTTER!

In 1880 Walter Camp, now a Yale alumnus, convinced Association that 11 men to a side would be better. Game was just one modification away from real progress.

In 1880 the field was reduced to 110 yards by 53 and "scrimmage" introduced, as opposed to Rugby's "scrum." In Rugby neither team had orderly possession. The ball had been tossed between two walls of rushers who mauled it around with their feet until it popped out to a free man. Now, one man was chosen to "heel" it back to a "quarterback," who could not run forward with it but who could maneuver it to other rushers to kick or run. The principle of possession of ball (and the idea of scrimmage) was, of course, mostly Walter Camp's, now the most influential man in the game.

The snapper-back in scrimmage became adept at flipping the ball back with his foot to start things off. A team was allowed to keep the ball for an entire half or until it scored. This provision, with possibility of stalemate, would lead to trouble.

Colleges in the South and Midwest were now playing the new game, and in 1881 Michigan made sports history with the first intersectional games, setting out to play Harvard, Yale, and Princeton in less than one week before returning home.

Professional trainers showed up that year at Eastern schools, and college administrators began to worry. Where would it all end?

Unfortunately, early rules permitted a team to hold the ball an entire half unless it punted or tried for a kicked goal from the field. In case of a scoreless tie in a "championship" game, the Association allowed the title to remain with the previous year's winner. So, a tie could be as rewarding as a victory. ●

Matters came to a head in 1881 in the famous Yale-Princeton "Block Game." Princeton held ball the entire first half without trying to score and Yale did likewise in second half. Result was complete boredom and the fans howled. ● ● ●

Once again the rules makers, urged by Camp, now coaching Yale, came to game's rescue. In 1882 another imaginative fundamental was added. Attacking team was required to advance ball five yards in three tries, or downs, or give it up. The football field took on its first striped appearance. ● ●

LEGS UP HIGH, JIM!

This led to the first signals, originally masked in casual phrases or a single word.

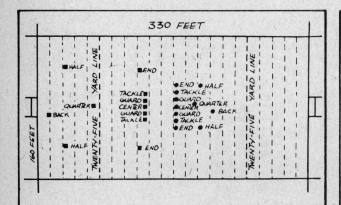

In 1882 came names of definite positions: seven forwards; quarterback; two halfbacks; fullback. Ends were at end of line. Next-to-end were called tackles because they made most stops on defense. Protectors of snapperback were guards.

The "downs" system of scrimmage brought an immediate new trend in personnel. The light, fast men who dominated the helter-skelter kicking and haphazard running offenses gave way to big men who began developing the short rushing offense needed to advance the ball five yards in three tries. Again, Yale started the trend, and by 1883 virtually every college switched to the running game. Kicking soon became mostly punting and the try after touchdown. In 1882, also, came the first eligibility rules limiting play to five years, getting rid of players who seemingly remained in college permanently. ● ●

Prior to 1883, scoring of a game was bitterly disputed. A field goal was superior to a touchdown but four touchdowns were better than one field goal. Players and fans argued relative values of field goal and try-after-touchdown. In case of a tie, a team with fewer safeties (which were non-scoring) was the winner. Obviously, the game would not be stabilized until something was done to adjust values of the varied scoring plays and keep them consistent in every game. ● ●

In the 1883 Association Meeting, Walter Camp (again!) devised first numerical scoring system: one point for safety; two for TD; four for try-after-touchdown; five for field goal.

But there were many fans who sensed that touchdowns would soon be more dramatic than goals kicked from field.

The season of 1884 introduced another great milestone—although soon a controversial one. Against Penn, Princeton turned up with the "V" trick, the forerunner of the flying wedge. In its eventual perfection, ten men formed a close V-shaped mass, with the ball-carrier in apex, forward. Once in motion the mass was hard to break through. It was first step toward putting real interference ahead of the runner, which was actually illegal at the time. In the beginning it was used only from a play from scrimmage. ● ●

Although there was a rule against interference ahead of the ball carrier, the violation, from 1884 on, kept cropping up so repeatedly that officials tacitly stopped calling it. (It would actually remain in the book until 1906 before being officially discarded.) Thus, with the flying wedge, the last vestige of Rugby melted away because in Rugby nobody could be ahead of ball carrier. At first, the wedge was used from scrimmage only, because there was no restriction on the number of men behind scrimmage line, and its momentum was somewhat limited by slow start.

But soon the wedge became almost standard maneuver on kickoffs. When executed properly it had fearful momentum, clearly was most dangerous play in game. It led to many serious injuries. Biggest heroes could smash through wedge.

Yale-Princeton game in 1886 was the first ever played on college grounds. It was the year's big social event.

THAT'S CUTTING HIM DOWN, JACK!

Probably biggest aid yet given the defense came in 1888 when tackling was allowed as low as knees. Previously, the ball carrier couldn't be hit below waist and now a smaller man could down the biggest, strongest of backs with crisp tackle.

By the late 1880s Yale had pioneered idea of swinging a line-man into line ahead of runner. A guard named George Wood-ruff (later great coach at Penn) was the first to do so. The defense promptly moved halfbacks up behind tackles. The strategic war of offense vs. defense was joined forever. ●

Public interest in the game increased still more in 1889 when sports authority Caspar Whitney chose first All-America: five from Princeton, three each from Harvard and Yale.

Prominent on the first honor team was Yale's tremendous 230-pound guard, Walter (Pudge) Heffelfinger, who special-ized in leading interference and smashing the flying wedge on defense. He became the most famed guard of all time.

Another selection was des-tined to become most famous coach and innovator in foot-ball history: Yale's 160-pound end, Amos Alonzo Stagg. ●

By 1890 every large school in the nation was playing football. High school administrators deplored the game and some tried to stop it. But there was no turning back American desire for contact sport. Incidentally, for protection, players were letting hair grow long and thick, resembling chrysanthemums.

By 1890 centers were snapping ball back with hands, instead of heeling it, and in 1892 Yale linemen stopped sparring with foe to get them off balance. Instead they eyed their center for the instant ball was snapped. It was such obvious improvement that rules were changed banning contact before snap.

First numerical signals had come in 1890. It led to cohesive offense—and cool, brainy quarterbacks who had to think fast in limited time.

George Woodruff, coaching Penn in early '90s, gave offense a boost with his new guard-back tactics. He put one, or both, in tandem behind point of attack, actually an improvement over wedge. This type of interference soon became popular attacking technique—but soon added to football's woes. ●

In early 1890s, guards back, flying wedge, and other momentum interference had begun to draw wide criticism from college heads and public. Football had become a brutal, injurious game. Many deaths made the '90s the Dark Age of sport.

First signs of a drawback came when West Point and Annapolis forbade their football teams to play anywhere but on their home grounds.

Rules in 1894 made drastic changes, banning all mass-momentum play. Not more than three men could start before ball was snapped, and couldn't be more than five yards back of ball, ending wedge from scrimmage (but not on kickoff).

Furthermore, offensive players no longer could use their hands while blocking foe, ending "knuckle" blocking.

In the early '90s, young Amos Alonzo Stagg, who'd been All-America at Yale and a great pitching prospect, had rejected baseball offers to go into coaching. After a year at Springfield (Mass.) YMCA, he took job at new U. of Chicago in 1892.

When Stagg took over at the raw "prairie" college, he had only 13 men, played himself in many of his team's games.

President William R. Harper lent prestige to the profession by making Stagg first paid coach with faculty status. Stagg became the West's first representative on football Rules Committee. ● ●

The canny young coach knew how to attract attention. In 1894 he startled the nation by traveling all the way to California to play Stanford (managed by future President, Herbert Hoover) and won, 28-0. For Stagg it was just the beginning as the Great Innovator. Football owes much to him.

Amos Alonzo Stagg originated spectacular end-around plays; reverses; and box defense in backfield.

Stagg also was the first coach to use crisscross plays and double hand-offs.

He also invented tackling dummy and was the first coach to put numbers on jerseys as aid for spectators.

Stagg was first to use fake place-kick in his early days, and later conceived the first man-in-motion play. He also originated the onside kickoff, still a common, dramatic maneuver by a trailing team to keep possession by recovering the ball.

A few years later, when the forward pass would be legalized, Stagg would be the first coach to develop it as an important and common part of his offense, instead of using it as an occasional novelty as most coaches would, at first. Such was the inventiveness of Stagg's mind that years later Knute Rockne would say: "All modern football comes from Stagg."

In 1895 football was in a major crisis. The Eastern Association was angrily split over mass play: Yale, Cornell, and Princeton were against it; Penn and Harvard for it. Two sets of rules were used that year. In fact, all college sports were in jeopardy, not just football, but football was chief offender.

Tramp athletes played football for one college, baseball for another, sometimes weren't enrolled in school.

College baseball teams often used professional pitchers, and as football began displacing baseball as top college sport, football games got so heated that college boys frequently were attacked by hostile "townies" after road games. The public became aroused and the press noted all incidents.

Although the East dictated rules, the Midwest took leadership morally. In 1895 President Smart of Purdue invited heads of Chicago, Michigan, Illinois, Wisconsin, Northwestern, and Minnesota to meet in Chicago to discuss leadership not only for football but all collegiate sports. It was the beginning of the Western Conference, later known as The Big Ten, first formally organized league.

The Midwest presidents who met in Chicago came up with a firm set of rules, including a three-year limit on varsity play; no freshman eligibility, tramp athletes, or training table; all athletic control to be by faculty. It was to set pattern for nation.

By mid-1890s uniforms were standardized. Moleskin pants had leather strips or fiber inside thigh. Laced canvas vests were worn over long-sleeved shirts of school colors. Cleats were now legal. Many players sewed leather buffer patches on jersey shoulders. First crude helmet didn't appear until 1896 and those who wore them were branded sissies. Consequently, few did. Ribs had no protection at all, nor did hips.

In 1895 Yale was the first team to use direct pass from center to kicker, eliminating long relay from quarterback.

In 1896 piling onto ball carrier was banned. So was flying wedge on kick-off. Mass play was further restricted by requiring at least five men on scrimmage line when ball was snapped. No offensive man could take more than one step without coming to stop before ball was snapped. The following year, in response to increasing popularity of running game, touchdowns were valued at five points, equal to field goal. A safety was worth two points and point-after was one point. And team captain now had privilege of substituting player at any time. Previously the referee granted permission.

HEISMAN WARNER HAUGHTON

At close of 19th century, football, though still in Dark Ages because of mass-play brutality, had already produced roots of great tradition and a crop of nationally famed players. Harvard-Yale had commenced their colorful series in 1875; Army-Navy in 1890. In addition to Stagg and Camp (who coached Yale, 1888-92, and then became rules leader) other men launched glittering careers. John Heisman, great Georgia Tech mentor for whom famed Trophy would be named, started at Oberlin in 1892. Glenn (Pop) Warner, famed at Carlisle Indian School, Pitt, and Stanford, debuted at Georgia in 1895 for $35 weekly. Percy Haughton, first of great Ivy leaders at Harvard, started his career at Cornell in 1899.

Knowlton (Snake) Ames, halfback on first All-America in 1889, won nickname and fame for his dodging skill.

Frank Hinkey, Yale's 145-pound end and deadliest tackler East had yet seen, was only player to make All-America four straight years, selected in 1891-94. ● ● ●

Phil King of Princeton, All-America in 1891-93, was regarded as first truly great quarterback-tactician. ● ●

T. Truxtun Hare, a three-time honor guard 1897-98-99, of Penn, was among most glamorized linemen of era. But the East was about to have its exclusivity on stardom cracked.

By 1898 East no longer could claim total supremacy in football. Three players from the Midwest cracked the national limelight. Wisconsin's legendary Pat O'Dea, an Australian, was probably the greatest kicker the game has produced. Frequently he drop-kicked goals of more than 60 yards. He was also a terrific fullback but despite his all-around brilliance he was, strangely enough, left off the All-America. But two other men from the Western Conference could not be overlooked for the honor.

Stagg developed a great fullback at Chicago, Clarence Herschberger; Michigan had Bill Cunningham, fine center. Midwest had broken through; other areas would follow.

But perhaps the first "real" All-America was Isaac Seneca, the great halfback from Carlisle, Pa., picked in 1899.

One of the most amazing stories of 1899 was tiny Sewanee College, at Sewanee, Tenn., stunning the nation by winning 12 straight over Georgia Tech, Georgia, Tennessee, Texas, Tulane, Louisiana State, Mississippi, Auburn, and others. Five of the games came in six days. Only Auburn scored on Sewanee. Even the East was impressed by backwoods heroes.

One of football's most colorful stories was that of Fielding H. ("Hurry-Up") Yost who came to Michigan in 1901, built his famed "Point-a-Minute" dynasty and saw his Wolverines labeled the most powerful teams the game had yet witnessed. In five seasons, 1901-05, Michigan rolled up 2821 points to 42; won 55, tied one, lost one (with 54 straight without defeat before an epic 2-0 loss to Stagg and Chicago). By retirement in 1927 Yost had developed 22 All-America players, more than any other coach in football history.

Yost's 1901 team was invited to Pasadena, Calif., to play Stanford in what was called the first Rose Bowl game, and creamed the Westerners, 49-0, on Jan. 1, 1902. Yost mercifully agreed to shorten the fourth quarter when he saw Stanford players' exhausted condition from Wolverines' power.

A hard-driving West Virginian, Yost earned famed nickname ("Hurry-Up") by his dynamic, speedy practice attitude. It became his label.

Among his many inventions was the spectacular Statue-of-Liberty play after introduction of forward pass in 1906.

Yost was first to use the tailback formation—inspired by talents of Wolverines' immortal halfback Willie Heston.

When Fielding Yost came to Michigan from San Jose, Calif., where he'd been coaching, he brought with him Willie Heston, a strong, stocky 190-pounder. Heston scored more than 100 touchdowns in 44 games for Point-a-Minute clubs.

So speedy was Heston that he frequently beat Archie Hahn, Michigan's Olympic champ, in short sprints.

Easily the nation's greatest running back of the early 20th century, Heston was famed for his lightning pivot plus devastating power, made All-America in 1903-04 seasons.

Customary defense of the day was nine-man line with two men in secondary. Heston's speed led to Minnesota forming radical seven-man line with four men dropped back to stop Heston when he burst through. It worked in 1903 and a 6-6 tie momentarily halted Point-a-Minute Express. Seven-man line became standard defense after that, lasting many years.

Although injuries and deaths were mounting, a clamor to open up the game in 1902 only partially succeeded. ●

The man who received the ball, usually the quarterback, now was allowed to run with it as long as he crossed scrimmage at least five yards from where ball was put in play. Lengthwise stripes were added to cross-stripes, making field look more like a huge rectangular checkerboard or a "gridiron."

But it wasn't enough. Under the system where only five yards were needed for a first down in three tries, mass play was still the vogue. Vicious slugging and kneeing were common and often went undetected. In the season of 1905 alone, 18 players were killed. College presidents were not organized to reverse the condition and the public was becoming revolted. Yet, the rules makers seemed paralyzed to act. Something — or someone — had to stir them into action.

It came with dramatic suddenness halfway through 1905 season. President Teddy Roosevelt summoned representatives of Harvard, Yale, and Princeton to White House and threatened to abolish the sport if they didn't press for removal of football's objectionable aspects leading to organized mayhem.

By the end of the 1905 season the outcry against football was heard from coast to coast. Teddy Roosevelt's threat was considered a very real thing. Northwestern and Union College revealed they would suspend the sport for a year and await developments. The president of the University of California sent a telegram to Eastern officials, saying: "The game of football must be made over or it must go." An announcement from President Nicholas Murray Butler, of Columbia, was even more dramatic. ●

Butler reported to the press that the faculty had decided to abolish football altogether. (It would not be restored there until 1915.) The game finally was in jeopardy. If something weren't done immediately there might not be a 1906 season.

As a result of impetus provided by Chancellor McCracken of New York University, 63 schools met on Dec. 28 and appointed committee to seek merger with the Football Rules Committee. From the merger came the Intercollegiate Athletic Assn. of U.S. (forerunner of prestigious N.C.A.A.). On Jan. 12, 1906, a new rules body, known as American Intercollegiate Football Rules Committee met and saved the sport. One idea would have the most profound effect yet on game.

In order to open up the game and provide safer football, the Rules Committee in 1906 came up with its most dramatic advance by putting in the forward pass, despite many restrictions on it. Among them: pass had to cross scrimmage line five yards out to either side of center snap. An incomplete pass could be recovered by either side if it had been touched. Pass caught behind goal line was touchback, not touchdown. Many critics thought pass too unsound. Throwing the squat, oval ball and catching it meant new skills.

But imaginative coaches realized its potential. First to put it to major use was Eddie Cochems at St. Louis University, where Brad Robinson was immediate success as thrower, Jack Schneider as receiver. They were said to be first to master the overhand spiral toss. The word traveled quickly.

In East, that first year of the pass, player designated to catch ball camped under a high, end-over-end lob. Teammates gathered around him to protect him from defense. Since an incomplete pass was a free ball when touched, Eastern coaches seldom passed that first year the ball was thrown.

But Cochems—and Stagg of Chicago — immediately sensed value of firing ball sharply to man running to certain spot. A year later everyone was tossing spiral.

The 1906 season marked end of fabled 3-year college career of Chicago's Walter Eckersall, who, along with Stagg, Yost, Heston, and Minnesota's Dr. Henry Williams, had swung football supremacy away from the East. Considered an all-time All-America quarterback of early football, Eckersall began as 125-pound QB for Hyde Park High in Chicago which, in 1901, took on and defeated Stagg's Chicago team. When "Eckie" enrolled at Chicago, Stagg didn't hesitate to install the then 140-pounder as varsity signal-caller as a soph. Eckersall ultimately became a great sports writer and famed as football referee in Midwest.

An All-America in 1904-05-06, Eckersall was a 9.8 Olympic sprinter, a devastating runner in open field, a brilliant strategist, punter, and drop-kicker. When pass came along in 1906 he was instantly adept, told Stagg first day: "It's a cinch!"

Eckersall was a field goal threat anywhere within 50-yard line; booted five each vs. Nebraska and Illinois. ●

A demon on defense, despite his size, he was only man ever to catch Willie Heston from behind. Eckersall's brilliance led to epic 2-0 win over Wolverines in '05 to end storied undefeated streak at 56 as Chicago tackled punt receiver in end zone.

In addition to putting in the forward pass in 1906, the new Rules Committee further opened up the game by requiring the offense to make 10 yards in three tries for a first down instead of five yards, which previously had been a great inducement for bruising, battering line play in which no form of mayhem was barred. Under the new rules, the quarterback now had to gamble with wide end sweeps and other wide-open plays. Action went over big with the public.

To further discourage mass play, at least six men were now required to be on offensive line. (This still permitted tackle or guard to take position behind line and enter an interference pattern, or an end to be part of ball-handling act.)

Hurdling, formerly cause of many serious injuries, was banned. Roughing penalties were put in. Incidentally, two years previously, field goal had been reduced from five to four points; for first time TD ranked over field goal.

In 1909 Yale, led by All-America fullback, Ted Coy, was finest team the East had yet produced. It not only was undefeated and unscored on but never allowed foe inside 25-yard line.

Coy, a two-year choice for All-America, was not only a great runner but probably the finest punter sport had seen.

That same year marked appearance of the Minnesota Shift, devised by coach Dr. Henry Williams, who played earlier with Stagg at Yale.

While teaching at Newburgh, N.Y. (before studying medicine), Williams had coached nearby Army team in 1891 by sending Cadets diagrams of plays. Occasionally he drove to nearby West Point in buggy to join team, and led Army to first win over Navy. But what he did at Minnesota brought real fame.

Dr. Henry L. Williams had arrived at Minnesota in 1900 with medical degree and an understanding he'd be permitted to continue medical practice while coaching. His first six years established Gophers as giant of football, winning 55, losing 4, tying 2, including epic 6-6 stand-off with mighty Michigan in 1903, stopping Willie Heston. From 1900 through 1905 his teams scored 2331 points to 115, with awesome 618 for 12 straight in 1904. In 1909 Williams' genius produced the famed Minnesota Shift. ●

Williams conceived idea of having team form tight group behind line, then springing into position instant before the snap. Defense had no time to judge direction or type of play. Entire backfield shift was a particularly effective maneuver. ● ●

In 1916 Walter Camp, scouting All-Americas, made first trip West to see a Big Ten team. Gophers were best in land. But lowly Illinois scored upset of decade, 14-9. Williams won eight Big Ten titles in 21 years before he retired in 1922.

Meanwhile, pass was in common use by now, but debate was rising over whether to limit the pass or free it from some existing restrictions.

In 1908, Wally Steffen, Chicago All-America QB, had developed run-or-pass feint. Soon all QBs did it, leading to a new imbalance in game.

Defensive secondaries, not knowing how to handle passes, backed far downfield, leaving tackles with no help. Terrific pounding of linemen almost ruined intent of game-opening passes. So new regulations were put in to restore a balance.

In 1910 mass play was completely banned by requiring seven men on offensive line. The restriction which allowed QB to run only if he went five yards to right or left of center snap was removed. Lengthwise stripes disappeared from the field.

No back could be aided by pushing or pulling, and the game was divided into quarters instead of halves.

With the pass still in its infancy, rules makers in 1910 wavered back and forth in legislating its use. Should they aid the aerial game—or limit it? It was not surprising that they went both ways—although in the main the pass benefited.

Ball had to be thrown from at least five yards behind scrimmage, but now it could cross line at any point rather than restricted to five yards to either side of center.

Distance of pass was now limited to not more than 20 yards from spot where the ball was put into play.

For the first time something was done to protect receiver. "Interference" would be called if offensive player were tackled, pushed, or prevented from attempting to catch ball. Formerly, it had been common to rough up receiver.

In 1912 the rules makers added improvements. Field was reduced from 110 yards to 100 yards, with an end zone behind each goal line. Kickoff was to be from the 40 instead of 55-yard line and a touchdown was now six points instead of five. (The field goal had been dropped from four to three a few years earlier and there no longer was any question about which was king: goal or TD.)

WOW! THAT MUST BE A 40-YARDER!

The forward pass also got new impetus when the 20-yard limitation was removed. The ball could now be tossed for any distance beyond the scrimmage line. Ends with speed were now in great demand to outrace the secondary defenders.

The offense got still another break when a fourth down was added in which a team could make a first down.

But perhaps the most dramatic change made in 1912 was legalizing touchdown on pass caught in end zone. Previously, a forward pass caught over goal line was a touchback and other team got the ball. The aerial game was now ready to take off—and two kids from Notre Dame would show how.

WE DON'T BELIEVE IN TOSSING IT AWAY!

Although the pass was widely used in early days, Eastern elevens seldom featured it in their offensive patterns.

Midwesterners were more imaginative. In summer of 1913 quarterback Gus Dorais and end Knute Rockne, of Notre Dame, worked at a Cedar Point, O., resort. They practiced on the Lake Erie beach, Dorais tossing and Rockne receiving.

Dorais, with deadly accuracy, and Rockne, among the first to master secret of catching with relaxed hands, were the first famed aerial combo. Army had scheduled little Notre Dame as a breather in 1913 but the East was stunned as Dorais completed 17 passes, mostly to Rockne, for an amazing 35-13 upset of Cadets. The East now knew it had to develop the pass to survive.

One of the game's greatest coaches was Glenn Scobey (Pop) Warner, a Cornell man who gained his first fame in early 20th century at Carlisle Indian School, Carlisle, Pa. Later he gained in stature at U. of Pittsburgh and Stanford.

Warner's most famous contribution was development of the double wingback, leading to spectacular reverses, tricky passing and other versatile open play. He was widely copied.

Warner is also said to have invented crouching start for backs and roll block, a big improvement over shoulder blocking in the open field. ●

Carlisle Indians, though undermanned, beat many of nation's best. They were great natural athletes and took well to Warner's deception. Once, Carlisle scored a TD on kickoff against Harvard when Charlie Dillon raced through befuddled Crimson team with ball concealed in the back of his jersey.

Warner's greatest player at Carlisle—and possibly greatest athlete in history — was Jim Thorpe, a Sac-Fox Indian.

As a boy in Oklahoma Territory, Thorpe had been a wrangler of wild horses. Sent to the Indian School at Carlisle the 6-foot, 190-pounder was an incredibly powerful runner who helped make Carlisle the football scourge of the East. He was a true triple-threat, equally adept in all skills and a great competitor.

All-America in 1911-12, he once drop-kicked four field goals vs. Harvard; was marvelous punter, deadly tackler. In 1912 he led nation's scorers with 25 TDs, 198 points.

A great baseball player and track star as well as footballer, Thorpe won the Olympic pentathlon and decathlon titles for the U.S. in 1912 Olympics but had to return his medals because he had briefly and innocently played a few pro baseball games in an obscure minor league. Later he played in the major leagues and was a terror in early years of pro football.

•Another great coaching figure of pre-World War I days was Harvard's Percy Haughton, who developed punting game as major offensive threat rather than defensive.

Haughton's punt protection was perfection itself, and he developed kickers who consistently bottled up opposition deep in their own territory. He stressed short passing game and only threw when Crimson crossed mid-field. Yet from 1908-16 his Harvard teams won 71, lost only 7, tied 5 to lead East.

RIP OFF THOSE FAKE BALLS OR I'LL PAINT THE FOOTBALL RED!

Harvard was unbeaten in 1912-14 as Haughton trained Charlie Brickley, legendary drop-kicker, who once booted five field goals vs. Yale.

It is said Harvard's 1914 team was greatest despite two ties. It featured Crimson immortal Eddie Mahan. A brilliant psychologist, Haughton threatened to paint game ball red when Pop Warner's Carlisle Indians showed up with tan football outlines sewn on their jerseys to confuse Harvard tacklers.

By World War I original Eastern powers and the Midwest were being forced to share the spotlight with newcomers. Pitt, under Pop Warner, was national champ in 1915; Georgia Tech, under John Heisman, in 1917. In 1915 Oklahoma had startled the nation not because it was undefeated in 10 games but because the Sooners gained more than a mile by passing, and scored 25 TDs on aerials, mostly by a famed combination of QB Forest Geyer and end Homer Montgomery).

Rose Bowl game was resumed in 1916 after initial effort in 1901 and would become most glamorous event in the sport. Washington State beat Brown, 14-0. The Easterners were led by halfback Fritz Pollard, in 1916 the first Negro All-America.

Paul Robeson, Rutgers end, was second Negro All-America in 1917. Later, he became world-famed opera singer.

REMEMBER--DON'T SAY A WORD UNTIL AFTER THE FIRST PLAY!

In 1917 a rule went into effect which prohibited a substitute from talking to teammates until one play had been completed, to prevent coaches from sending in a special play from bench.

Newest national power to rise before World War I was Ohio State, led by mercurial Chic Harley, 160-pound halfback who was Walter Camp's first sophomore All-America since game went "modern" in 1906 with introduction of the pass.

Buckeyes were undefeated in 1916-17 as Harley ran wild in every game and drop-kicked sensational field goals. In Big Ten debut on muddy field against Illinois in 1916 he raced for tying touchdown in final period; then, taking off mud-caked shoe he called for dry one and calmly kicked point that started Ohio State on three-year era of national grid fame.

After military service, Harley returned in 1919 for what surely would be third straight undefeated season.... ●● ●

OH, NO! HOW COULD THIS HAPPEN TO HARLEY?

But fate was in the wings. Until 1919 finale with Illinois, Harley had never played in losing game; in his three All-America years he'd scored more than half his team's points! In last 10 seconds Illini's Bob Fletcher booted field goal for 9-7 win in the most dramatic grid upset of many seasons. ●● ●

Following Harley, another star rose in Midwest as a legend was born at Notre Dame. George Gipp, called by Knute Rockne the greatest player he'd ever coached, had never played in high school, was ordered by Rockne in 1916 to report to frosh squad when he saw Gipp punting 60 yards to a friend on campus lawn. Next year he was on Irish varsity.

Daring and confident, Gipp tipped off his nature by ignoring punt signal in one game and coolly drop-kicking 55-yard field goal. ● ●

Six-feet-2, and 185 pounds, Gipp was also a great passer and slashing runner, led Irish to two straight unbeaten years (1919-1920), launching Notre Dame as brightest symbol of gridiron glamour. ●

Gipp was All-America in 1920 but had played with sore throat against Northwestern in final game and died shortly after of infection. Legend has it that as he was dying he told Rockne to tell team some day, when behind, to "win one for the Gipper." Trailing Army a few years later, Rockne did so and Notre Dame came on to "win one for the Gipper." ● ● ●

The early 1920s abounded in success stories as fans fed upon the postwar football boom. Honors were spread over widely varied places. Lafayette and Washington & Jefferson were other small colleges with towering achievements. W. & J. first drew national attention in 1919 with selection of Wilbur (Fats) Henry as All-America tackle. Its 1921 club, led by All-America tackle Russ Stein, held mighty California to scoreless tie in Rose Bowl, Jan. 1, 1922, and was claimant of national championship.

Lafayette, under the young Jock Sutherland, was as good as there was. In 1921, unbeaten Leopards were acknowledged big-time power, led by crack end Charley Berry (later famed big league umpire) and Frank Schwab, All-America guard.

Howard Jones, ex-Yale star and brother of fabled Tad Jones, made Iowa national power in 1921-22 with brilliant undefeated teams. ●

The corn-fed Hawkeyes had stars galore in triple-threat All-America QB Aubrey Devine; All-America FB Gordon Locke; and great Negro tackle, Duke Slater, whom everyone claimed was overlooked as AA, and later became a Federal Judge in Chicago. Slater was noted for playing without helmet. ● ●

Among the dramatic chapters of football in the early 1920s had been the story of little Centre College of Danville, Ky. The student body of 295 included three Texans: Bo McMillin, Red Roberts, and Jim Weaver, recruited by coach Charley Moran, veteran Big League umpire, who led Centre gridders in his off-season. The "Praying Colonels," as they were called, startled the nation's fans after a fine 1919 season by wangling two games with mighty Harvard for 1920-21, and immediately proceeded to make gridiron history.

The country boys were over-awed by the spectacle of Soldier Field in Cambridge, got drubbed 34-13 in the first game. Fans laughed when Centre's triple-threat QB Bo McMillin defiantly snarled: "We'll be back here next year to take you!"

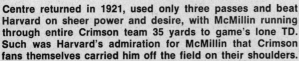

Centre returned in 1921, used only three passes and beat Harvard on sheer power and desire, with McMillin running through entire Crimson team 35 yards to game's lone TD. Such was Harvard's admiration for McMillin that Crimson fans themselves carried him off the field on their shoulders.

Centre was the smallest college ever to turn out All-Americans, in McMillin and James (Red) Roberts, an end.

WE CAN'T POSSIBLY WIN. FOUR MEN ARE INJURED... AND THERE ISN'T A REAL STAR ON THE CLUB.

No mention of grid success in postwar years would be valid without "Gloomy Gil" Dobie and great unbeaten Cornell clubs of 1921-22-23, scoring 1070 points to 81. ●

Dobie, a Minnesota star, previously had phenomenal years at U. of Washington with 58 wins and three ties in 61 games. At Cornell he became a titan of the East. His nickname stemmed from perennial pessimism and skepticism over his chances.

Hallmark of Dobie's finesse was his brilliant concept of double-wing attack. Big Red team of 1922 was probably his best. It featured All-America HB Eddie Kaw; QB George Pfann and tackles Leonard Hanson and Frank Sundstrom.

PFANN

In 1923 Sundstrom and Pfann were All-America. Pfann, a powerful runner, smart play-caller, was Rhodes scholar.

Yale's unbeaten team of 1923, coached by fabled Tad Jones, was one of game's greatest. It had brightest galaxy of stars of any modern Ivy club, including Bill Mallory, All-America HB; All-America tackle Century Milstead; Win Lovejoy and Dick Luman (who were AA center and guard the next year); Mal Stevens, and Ducky Pond, who later coached the Eli's.

Six were transfers. (Milstead from Wabash, Stevens from Washburn, Widdy Neale from West Virginia, and others.) Ducky Pond got his nickname sloshing in mud 67 yards with fumble for first TD vs. Harvard in seven years.

An amazingly fast and alert team, Eli's recovered 23 of their foes' 27 fumbles during the season, scored 230 points to 38 in eight games. ● ●

Tad Jones delivered one of the most quoted lines in football history before Harvard game. "Gentlemen, you are about to play football for Yale against Harvard. Never in your lives will you ever do anything so important!" They all believed it.

The story of Knute Kenneth Rockne of Notre Dame is a saga that belongs to all football. He rose from Norwegian immigrant boy to the pinnacle of coaching success. ● ●

Rockne, who'd captained Irish in 1913, became head coach in 1918 and also taught chemistry. Soon he gave up lab to concentrate on football as Notre Dame became most-traveled and colorful team in nation—and the most successful. ● ●

Rockne always claimed every play was a touchdown play if every man carried out his blocking chore perfectly.

Notre Dame under Rockne made brilliant use of the pass but it was famed Notre Dame Shift which high-lighted the Irish striking power—and was probably the most discussed adjunct of Rockne's genius. (Next: the controversial shift.) ● ● ●

Although shift was an old maneuver, Rockne perfected it. From set, modified T formation, the four backs hopped rhythmically into a box formation a split second before snap. It kept defense off-balance and lent a certain momentum even though backs were required to come to full stop. But extent of "full stop" was the controversial item. The shift was widely imitated throughout the nation amid furor that it was illegal.

Shifting quickly out of set positions gave defense no chance to read formation as to whether it was square, V, Z, flanker; no time to look for back tipping off play; or even whether quarterback would handle the football first.

Rockne was master psychologist. Once, ill, in wheelchair, with Irish trailing, he rolled into dressing room between halves and with two-minute pep talk sent team back out to beat U.S.C, 13-12. Another time, upset by poor play, he threatened to leave bench and sit in stands as spectator. Again the needle worked and Notre Dame roared back to win.

Rockne's most famous team featured fabled "Four Horsemen," who first started as soph unit late in 1922. What followed in 1923-24 seasons was football immortality . . .

MILLER   LAYDEN   CROWLEY   STUHLDREHER

In 1924 after Notre Dame had crushed a great Army team in New York, sportswriter Grantland Rice wrote: "Outlined against a blue-gray October sky, the Four Horsemen rode again. Not as War, Famine, Pestilence and Death, but as Stuhldreher, Miller, Crowley and Layden. . . ." Two days later a publicity man in South Bend posed them on horses and the photo blanketed the nation's press. The nickname for the foursome became one of the lasting legends of the sport.

The Four Horsemen averaged only 165 pounds but timing and skill made them most versatile backfield yet seen, operating behind a great line called the "Seven Mules."

With Harry Stuhldreher, QB; Don Miller and Jim Crowley at HB; and Elmer Layden, FB, Notre Dame was upset only by Nebraska in 1923, was undefeated in 1924. They closed their career Jan. 1, 1925, with smashing 27-10 Rose Bowl victory over Stanford, led by the great Ernie Nevers. In their two big years, the high-geared Irish scored 560 points to foe's 91.

Bob Zuppke, one of the most colorful and imaginative coaches in history, never played college football (but played basketball at Wisconsin). Yet he became high school grid coach, made Oak Park, Chicago, a national power. He moved up to Illinois in 1913 and became an instant and huge success.

Zuppke's Illini won seven Big Ten, three national titles in first 16 years but refused to get involved with high-pressure recruiting in early 1930s. He made up in genius what he lacked in material, and football owes much to him. ● ●

In his early high school coaching days Zuppke devised spiral snap from center as opposed to slower end-over-end flip which was often blocked on the punter. ●

Zuppke invented screen pass, and in 1922 used first huddle instead of barking signals at line, which often were garbled. His 29 years at Illinois made him second only to Stagg in Big Ten service—and he developed most famous player in football history: The Galloping Ghost—No. 77—Red Grange.

Red Grange, football's most glamorous player, went out for frosh team at Illinois in 1922, was so dismayed by competition he quit after first day. Fraternity brothers said they'd paddle him if he didn't go back. Grange did, immediately ran wild through entire varsity in first scrimmage.

Grange debuted in 1923, was instant All-America. He was fast but it was his incredible change of pace, balance, and reactions which made him football's most exciting runner. He missed a few games with injuries but in 20 college games he scored 31 TDs, ran for record 3637 yards and even completed 42 passes from his HB position to prove his versatility.

Publicity built up around him: he was known as "The Wheaton Iceman," from summer work in home town. Every high school gridder suddenly wanted job on ice wagon.

In October, 1924, when Illinois dedicated new stadium, Grange turned in the most spectacular performance in grid annals. Against Michigan he raced for four TDs on long runs of 95, 67, 56, and 44 yards the first four times he touched the ball, in only 11 minutes; tallied another later on, passed for a sixth, had total of 402 yards running in smashing 39-14 victory.

YEP. AND ALL GALLI - CURCI CAN DO IS SING!

THERE'S NEVER BEEN ANYONE LIKE HIM!

As Grange's fame spread, a sports writer sneered to Bob Zuppke that all the 175-pound Redhead could do was run. Zup's caustic reply referred to greatest opera star of day.

Midway through Grange's fabled career Grantland Rice again used poetic lines to make a national symbol: "A streak of fire, a breath of flame / Eluding all who reach and clutch / A gray ghost thrown into the game / That rival hands may never touch." And the Galloping Ghost was born. But, strangely, Eastern critics weren't convinced that Red was for real.

Grange, whose No. 77 was most-famed ever worn and was first to be retired by any college, convinced Easterners when Illini played Penn at Franklin Field in mud, and slithered through and around Quakers for 363 yards and three TDs.

Pro football, struggling to survive its early years, was saved when Grange signed for series of games with the Chicago Bears after his final college season ended in 1925. ● ●

By the 1920s football was the truly great collegiate sport. Tremendous stadiums began to rise. Harvard had been the first (1903), then Yale (1913). Now, after World War I, Ohio State built its huge concrete horseshoe, followed by Illinois, and the era of commercialized college football was born. Intensive recruiting and the various evils that accompanied a win-or-else philosophy would make football a troubled high-pressure sport.

Technical excellence was spreading. John W. Heisman, an old-time Penn star, was the father of Southern football while at Georgia Tech, 1904-19, and contributed much to the game. Later, the famed Heisman Trophy would be awarded in his memory as a brilliant gridiron tactician and sportsman.

WADE

In 1922, Wallace Wade, a Tennessean who'd starred on Brown's Rose Bowl team in 1915, began coaching at Alabama and made the nation Southern-football-conscious when the Crimson Tide in 1926 became first Dixie club to play in Rose Bowl. 'Bama, led by sensational halfback Johnny Mack Brown, beat Washington and started a stream of Southern schools toward Pasadena. Brown, a handsome athlete, went to Hollywood the following year, became a cowboy movie star.

The Southwest produced the first "razzle-dazzle" football, with coaches taking advantage of mild weather to develop wild passing game. Southern Methodist, for 15 years under Ray Morrision, became known nationally as "Aerial Circus."

On the West Coast, Andrew L. (Andy) Smith made the nation aware of his U. of California "Wonder Bears," undefeated five straight seasons, 1920-24, winning 45 games and tying three, and playing twice in Rose Bowl.

California smashed Ohio State, 28-0, in the 1921 Bowl game to really put the Coast League on the gridiron map. Feature of the contest was 65-yard touchdown pass completed by Brick Muller, Bear end who often dropped back to throw. It was reported to be the longest pass in Rose Bowl history.

The next season, Muller led Bears to second straight Bowl game, a crunching scoreless tie with Washington & Jefferson, a small Eastern school that had become a national power. Muller was first Coast All-America—but many would follow in Muller's footsteps.

First universally-acclaimed Coast glamor star was Ernie Nevers of Stanford. His coach, Pop Warner, who'd also had Jim Thorpe at Carlisle, claimed Nevers was better than Thorpe. A 200-pounder, raised in Wisconsin, Nevers went West to become one of game's all-time great fullbacks, 1923-24-25, and All-America in senior year when he led Cardinals to first win over California in 20 years. He was not only a pulverizing line-blaster and blocker but one of the best punters of 1920s.

An amazingly versatile athlete, Nevers also excelled in basketball, baseball, and track, in which he threw the javelin and shot. When he graduated in June, 1926, the blond thunderbolt had to make a career choice: professional baseball or football.

He was a good enough pitcher to win in the American League but soon gave it up to play pro football.

58

In 1925 Michigan's Big Ten champs featured the most famous aerial combination of all time: QB Benny Friedman throwing to End Benny Oosterbaan. They sparked what "Hurry-Up" Yost called his greatest team (227 points to three). All-America in 1925-26 they were the only forward passing duo ever to make All-America two straight years. Friedman was 5-11, 175; Oosterbaan 6-2, 195.

FRIEDMAN   OOSTERBAAN

Friedman, a brainy field general, was finest passer the game had yet produced, and was first QB to use pass on first down and as consistent weapon instead of mere adjunct to running game. Oosterbaan had speed, remarkable hands and was first end to develop repertoire of faking moves on secondary.

TIGHT AGAINST THE SIDELINE, BENNY!

They had uncanny knack of finding holes in defense, picked precise spots on field for their pass completions.

Also the best place-kicker of his day, Friedman booted many game-winning field goals. In 1925 he beat Illinois and Red Grange, 3-0, and in 1926 his 50-yarder vs. Ohio State gave Wolves title again.

Oosterbaan was All-America again in 1927 after Friedman graduated; was first modern wingman to make it three straight years. He was also All-America basketballer.

59

Mayes McClain, big Indian fullback from Haskell Institute, set all-time modern scoring mark in 1926: 253 points on 38 TDs, 19 PATs, two field goals in 11 games. (following year he transferred to and starred for Iowa.) Also, in 1926, Brown University came up with famed "Iron Men." Under Tuss McLaughry, Bruins used single- and double-wing and unorthodox 7-2-2 defense, won nine, tied one and astounded grid world with their stamina.

In key Yale and Dartmouth games on successive Saturdays, Brown used only 11 original starters. Two weeks later vs. Harvard, two subs played last four minutes. In wind-up tie contest with Colgate, Brown used only 12 men.

Stars were All-America QB Roy Randall; HBs Al Cornsweet and Dave Mishel, with the latter forming a great pass combination with End Hal Broda. Orland Smith was great tackle.

But the real physical marvel of late 1920s was the player who was truly a legend in his time, a Ukrainian Viking from University of Minnesota . . .

Bronko Nagurski (a real Ukrainian first name, not nickname), born in Rainy Lake, Ont., Canada, was "Paul Bunyan" of football. Minnesota star of 1927-28-29 was cyclonic 220-pounder with amazing strength and quickness, and virtually indestructible. At small Minnesota high school he played football, basketball, was all-around track ace, but arrived on Gopher campus absolutely unknown. The Minnesota grid coaches drooled, weren't sure how to use him.

As soph he played end, tackle and guard, but mostly tackle. It was said opposition never gained more than five yards in entire game, through or over him. He was forever smashing interference and nailing the runner. Coaches kept wondering how this big, tough athlete would do as fullback. ●●●

As junior he played tackle on defense, fullback on offense. Lone tackler couldn't stop him. Once he played with special brace protecting three broken ribs. ●●●

In days before Big Ten scholarships, Bronko worked way through school as night-watchman, waiter-bouncer in restaurant. In 1929 one All-America team named only 10 men; Nagurski was used at two positions: at fullback and tackle.

FESLER   CAGLE   STRONG   CLARK

Other stars of the late 1920s included versatile Wes Fesler, Ohio State three-time All-America end, 1928-29-30, and basketball and baseball star; Chris Cagle, brilliant Army All-America HB, 1928-29; Ken Strong, NYU All-America FB and tremendous kicker, 1928; Earl (Dutch) Clark, unheralded HB from Colorado College and Rocky Mountain area's first A-A, 1928; and Pest Welch, 195-pound triple-threat All-America HB and star of great Purdue club of 1929. ●●●

Meanwhile, subsidizing and proselytizing of college stars was becoming alarming. Carnegie Foundation went so far as to issue widely-publicized "Carnegie Report" blasting game and administrators, revealing serious abuses. Repercussions and needed reforms would soon be evidenced all over.

Biggest scandal was at Iowa, in 1929, where financial irregularities connected with All-America HB Willis Glasgow brought the first and only suspension of a school from a college conference. Big Ten dropped the Hawkeyes for a year. ●

While personalities were adding to game's glitter in the 1920s, the rules makers were being active, too. The point-after had previously been from the 5-yard line at a spot opposite where TD had crossed goal line. In 1922 it was spotted on the five but in front of goal posts, doing away with wide-angled tries.

In 1925, in effort to cut down injuries, clipping (blocking from behind) was made illegal and penalized 15 yards.

In 1926, pass was restricted by 5-yard penalty and loss of down for two incompletes in same series of downs.

In 1927 a dramatic move was made, affecting field goals and PATs, when goal posts were taken off goal line and placed at rear of end zone.

The legend of "Win one for the Gipper," was climaxed in 1928 at the Polo Grounds in New York when a great Army team led by Chris Cagle was leading sub-par Notre Dame. (A four-time loser that year.) Between halves, Rockne recalled for his dispirited troops George Gipp's death-bed request: "Some day, Rock, when the going is real tough, ask 'em to win one for the Gipper . . ."

Irish, trailing at halftime, left dressing room all charged up. Late in game, Jack Chevigny, smashing over for the winning TD in a 12-6 upset, cried: "This one's for the Gipper!" It salvaged Rockne's worst season as Notre Dame football coach.

Game lost some familiar drama in 1929 on new fumble rule. When recovered by opponents after hitting ground, fumble now could not be advanced past that spot.

Biggest crowd ever at football game — 123,000 — packed Soldiers Field, Chicago, Nov. 16, 1929, to see Notre Dame beat Southern Cal, 13-12. It was the first of two back-to-back seasons which were to be Rockne's peak of perfection.

Football's most spectacular goof was made by a fine Univ. of California center, Roy Riegels, in Rose Bowl game vs. Georgia Tech on Jan. 1, 1929. Riegels would be forever famed for his dramatic wrong-way run with the ball.

Scooping up Tech fumble on Cal 40, Riegels was hit, spun around two or three times, and, finding himself free, took off for goal-line. But it was wrong goal. Team-mate Benny Lom pursued him, screaming, pulled him down on own 2-yard line.

Riegels, stunned by mistake, was consoled by teammates, stayed in to center ball on Cal punt from own end-zone. ●

Riegel's snap to Lom, the punter, was erratic. Tech blocked the kick for safety, and the two-pointer was the margin of victory as Yellow Jackets went on to win the bizarre Bowl game, 8-7. ●

The 1930 season brought "legislation against Notre Dame," as Rockne termed it. His shift had become too popular, and rules makers decided there must be full stop of at least one second before snap. New rule killed off all momentum and element of surprise. But it didn't stop Irish, national champs the previous year and now, again, in 1930, with eight men from the two teams named All-America between 1929 and 1931. Critics said 1930 club was better than Four Horsemen team.

Rockne set new style with swift, 160-pound All-America "watch-charm" guards, Jack Cannon, Bert Metzger. Other All-Americas: Tackles Joe Kurth, Nordy Hoffman; center Tommy Yarr. But the toast of football was his backfield . . .

CARIDEO

SCHWARTZ

BRILL

Frank Carideo, at QB, was great kicker, passer and tactician. Marchmont Schwartz was nation's most brilliant HB; Marty Brill at other HB was power runner and tremendous blocker. All three were All-America in 1930. Joe Savoldi and Moon Mullins were FB. Unit had as much talent as Four Horsemen—and were much bigger. By now, Notre Dame was supreme box-office lure in the land, traveled so widely they were also known as Ramblers. But school banned Rose Bowl appearances.

On March 31, 1931 a plane crashed in a Kansas cornfield, killing all passengers, including Knute Kenneth Rockne, who was only 43 at the time. Football, about to enter a new era in the 1930s, suffered an irreplaceable loss felt throughout the nation. Even the President of the U.S. was notified immediately of the disaster which took the life of the most glamorous and successful football coach the game had ever known. There would be other great coaches, but never another Rockne.

"Victory goes not only to the strong and brave but to boys who think. Football is played with the arms, legs and shoulders—but mostly above the neck!"
—Knute Rockne.

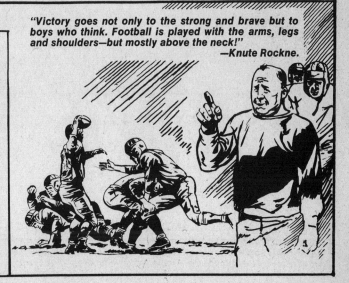

His background alone made him unique: an immigrant Norwegian boy who worked as railroad brakeman and mail clerk for five years before entering Notre Dame as student at age 22. His record as coach made him symbol of superiority without peer. In 13 years he won 105, lost only 12, tied five for best mark of any major coach during like period of time. Five of his 13 teams were undefeated; six lost only once. He turned out 13 All-Americas. His impact of personality was tremendous. More than anything else he was stamped by his intellectual and spiritual approach to the game of football.

The 1930s gave the game a new look. The ball was re-styled, slimmer, more pointed, to help the passer—who got further aid by elimination of penalty for two incompletes in same series of downs. Over-all the decade was marked by particularly fine teams, glittering superstars, notable individual games—and the definite emergence of pro football, previously a precarious enterprise, as something fans would support. Most exciting game of early 30s was drama-packed Notre Dame-Southern Cal meeting at South Bend.

Irish had gone three seasons, 25 games without loss, led by Marchy Schwartz, All-America HB; and Tommy Yarr, A-A center. Hunk Anderson, taking over after Rockne's death, was a first-year hero. Now, late in November, 1931, Howard Jones was bringing in great but underdog U.S.C. for titanic clash.

SHAVER   PINCKERT   ROSENBERG

The hard-running, crisp-blocking Trojans were star-studded: QB Gaius Shaver; HB Ernie Pinckert; Guards John Baker, Aaron Rosenberg; Tackle Ernie Smith; End Garrett Arbelbide. But brilliant Irish efficiency seemed more than match for them.

Notre Dame got out in front and led 14-0 as fourth quarter started. It was shaping up as romp, and a third straight Irish national championship...

Trailing Notre Dame 14-0 in fourth quarter, U.S.C. in 1931 refused to fold in one of all-time great games. Trojans drove 47 yards with Gus Shaver going over. But Joe Kurth, Irish All-America tackle, blocked John Baker's PAT.

Soon, Trojans marched again, 57 yards, Shaver scoring a second time. This time Baker made PAT. With time fading, and trailing 14-13, U.S.C. got ball again, four minutes left.

A 50-yard pass, Mohler to Arbelbide, first Trojan completion of day, was big play in drive to Irish 33, fourth down, less than a minute left. Atoning for missed PAT, Baker booted field goal for 16-14 win and national championship. HBs Shaver and Ernie Pinckert, and Baker, were All-America. The following year with unbeaten season, Jones' Trojans again dominated college grid. Tackle Ernie Smith and Guard Aaron Rosenberg, later famed movie producer, were All-America.

KIPKE

Spotlighted in early 1930s were great Michigan teams of Coach Harry Kipke. In four years, (1930-31-32-33), Wolverines lost only once. Unbeaten team of 1932 featured stocky All-America QB Harry Newman, great passer-kicker-runner.

Coach Andy Kerr, at Colgate, brilliant exponent of the double-wing attack and faultless ball-handling, came up with a rarity. Kerr, who had made Colgate an Eastern power in the late 1920s, reached a hotly-discussed pinnacle in 1932 season.

In 1929 and again in '30, Kerr's Red Raiders had held seven foes scoreless. In '31 they did it five times. But in nine games in 1932 Colgate was unbeaten, untied, unscored upon—and "uninvited." Many fans throughtout the country thought this great Colgate team, which had racked up 254 points, should have been invited to Rose Bowl, instead of twice-tied Pitt which lost to U.S.C.

THORNHILL

LITTLE

Eastern football, on the wane by the 1930s, got a lift from a great Columbia team in 1933 when Lions, coached by Lou Little, lost only to Princeton in upset, astounded fans by being invited by Stanford to Rose Bowl. Indians, led by Tiny Thornhill, were famed "Vow Boys," a great group who as frosh, vowed never lose to hated rival, USC—and never did. In their three varsity years (1933-34-35) Vow Boys, led by All-America HB Bobby Grayson and A-A tackle, Bob Reynolds, lost only two games, vs. Washington, 6-0, and UCLA, 7-6.

Thus, nation's fans jeered at 1934 Rose Bowl game as mismatch. Though Columbia had All-America QB Cliff Montgomery and fine first team, it had absolutely no depth. But Lions had perhaps most publicized of all plays—KF-79.

Jan. 1, 1934 came up drizzly and muddy. Six times Stanford drove within 10-yard line—six times were stopped by frenzied Lion defense. Then, after Montgomery completed the only Columbia pass of day to Red Matal on Stanford 17, Lions made history. Montgomery swept right, handed off to Al Barabas going left, who pretended he was merely faking, hid ball on hip, then loped 17 yards around befuddled Indians for TD and 7-0 upset. (First win by Eastern team in 15 years.)

Reigning Southern coach in early 30s was Alabama's Frank Thomas, QB of Rockne's first ND team. Thomas came to 'Bama in 1931, won 115, lost 24, tied seven before retiring in 1946. He had four unbeaten teams, took Crimson Tide to three Rose Bowls.

"Stars Fell on Alabama" was the big popular song of 1934—and it lit up 'Bama team, too. HB Dixie Howell-to-End Don Hutson was most glamorous aerial duo of decade. Bill Lee was great tackle and Riley Smith terrific QB. ● ● ● ●

In Rose Bowl, Jan. 1, 1935, The Tide rolled over Washington State as Howell scored two TDs, passed to Hutson for two more. Hudson later was record pass-receiver with Packers.

Opposite Hutson was a fine flanker who later on was humorously referred to simply as "the other end." His name: Paul (Bear) Bryant. ● ●

Among other items, 1935 provided two dramatic highlights. In one of greatest college games ever played, undefeated Ohio State met unbeaten Notre Dame in a titanic battle which, the experts said, would decide the unofficial national championship. The star-studded Buckeyes completely stifled the Irish, held a 13-0 lead going into the fourth quarter. But Notre Dame put on an epic last-period rally to score three touchdowns for an 18-13 victory, the final TD coming with 20 seconds left.

A Bill Shakespeare-to-Wayne Milner pass in end zone scored the winning TD as Notre Dame star, Andy Pilney, injured earlier while sparking the final drive, raised up from stretcher to witness the play. Emotionally drained and exhausted, Irish were upset the following week by Northwestern, 14-7.

This was debuting year of Heisman Award. First winner was a super-star who had played three years (1933-34-35) for a very weak Chicago team: Jay Berwanger, a 6-foot, 200-pound quadruple threat halfback for Maroon.

All-America in 1934-35 while Chicago was winning eight, losing eight, Berwanger always played with iron mask because of chronic nose injury. He did Maroon passing, punting, kicking-off, PATs; carried 439 times in 23 games for 1839 yards, scored 22 TDs, was ferocious blocker and defensive player. Critics said he was best all-around back since Jim Thorpe.

When Bernie Bierman went off to war in 1943, he left behind at Minnesota what many considered greatest 10-year coaching record in grid history. From 1933 when he came up from Tulane, his record with Gophers showed 63-12-5; five undefeated seasons (1933-34-35-40-41); five national championships (1934-35-36-40-41; and only coach in history to win three national crowns in row); seven Big Ten titles and 15 All-Americas. He had one winning streak of 21, another of 19. (A record later to be broken by one of his pupils.)

Bierman as boy overcame chronic bone disease to captain great Minnesota club of 1915. As coach of Alma Mater his single-wing power game was hailed as distinct grid era in itself. He forged mobile lines, and versatile backfields.

BEVAN

LARSON

LUND

WIDSETH

Bierman's undefeated 1934 team was declared by critics to be the greatest yet seen in grid annals, scored 270 points to 38 in eight games, produced four All-America players, led by triple-threat HB Pug Lund. Others: End Frank Larson; Tackle Ed Widseth; Guard Bill Bevan, who played without helmet.

Unbeaten again in 1935, Bierman's Vikings continued into '36 with 21 straight wins. Then, on muddy Northwestern field, stage was set for high, unforgettable drama.

74

In 1936 mighty Minnesota found itself held scoreless in the mud at Northwestern for three quarters. Then, when a 15-yard penalty against the Gophers for roughing put the ball on the one-yard line, Wildcats punched it over, ending Bernie Bierman's first brilliant winning streak at 21 games. ● ● ●

This game, plus outstanding job in his second year at Northwestern, brought Lynn (Pappy) Waldorf acclaim as Coach-of-Year in first annual vote for coaching honors.

Among Minnesota stars was Charles (Bud) Wilkinson, whom Bierman converted from potential All-America guard to a smart, blocking QB. Later, Wilkinson would make history at Oklahoma.

Bierman subsequently launched a new winning streak late in 1939 and carried over to back-to-back undefeated national title seasons of 1940-41 for 19 straight. So awesome was Minnesota's power he won 1940 Big Ten championship in key game with Ohio State without attempting a single pass! ●

Texas Christian supplied two straight glamor QBs in the 1930s, both exceptional passers who, under Coach Leo (Dutch) Meyer, gave tremendous impetus to the modern aerial game, aided by the slimmer ball developed in 1934. First, in 1935-36, came All-America Slinging Sammy Baugh, 6-4, 180. After him came little Davey O'Brien in 1937-38, only 5-7, 152.

Baugh led Horned Frogs to 11-1 season in '35; 8-2-2 in 1936, and the way he riddled defenses with his stand-up slinging was the talk of the nation. He became a great pro with the Washington Redskins, operating out of the single wing.

O'BRIEN

A stubby squirmer, O'Brien in 1937-38 fired ball like a bullet, often on the run. TCU's 1938 team, 10-0, was Southwest Conference's greatest to date, with O'Brien completing more than 50% of tosses, and Ki Aldrich, center, both All-America. The mercurial O'Brien also a fine runner and kicker, won Heisman Trophy, later was FBI man after starring as pro with Eagles.

Rules in 1937 brought compulsory numbers front and rear; ball was brought in when dead 15 yards from sidelines. Helmets were made mandatory in 1939.

John Bain Sutherland, Scottish-born, was star at Pitt, became dentist, then took on coaching job at Alma Mater to become one of game's all-time greats. From 1924 to 1948 he posted record of 111-20-12, had four unbeaten teams, four trips to Rose Bowl. He made Pitt the top Independent team of his day, beat Notre Dame six of seven times, 1932-37; limited the Irish to only 15 points in his six victories over them. ●

SUTHERLAND

Sutherland was fundamentalist, seldom passed, developed football's finest ground game. He got terrific power from single-wing and deep reverse. His pulling guards were so meticulously drilled he would examine tracks on grass to point out error in inches in path taken by the interferers. ●

Pitt teams of 1935-36-37 played unique three straight scoreless stand-offs with mighty Fordham, featuring Seven-Blocks-of-Granite including Vince Lombardi.

Sutherland's 18 All-Americas in 15 years of single-platoon football is record for modern coaches. Greatest team was unbeaten '37 club with so-called "Dream Backfield:" QB John Michelosen; HBs Marshall Goldberg, John Stebbins; FB Frank Patrick and Bill Stapulis. Sutherland resigned after 1938 season, protesting Pitt's "de-emphasis" of football. ●

Greatest athlete ever from Rocky Mountain area was Colorado's Byron (Whizzer) White, unanimous All-America HB of 1937 season.

White, a 6-foot, 195-pound slashing runner, led the nation's scorers with 16 TDs, 23 PATs. He also passed from his tailback position, averaged phenomenal 43.3 per punt; returned 36 punts for 731 yards; and also called the signals. ● ●

Called "Whizzer," with good reason, he was all-conference choice in basketball, baseball; made Phi Beta Kappa and went to Oxford as Rhodes Scholar. Returning to U.S., with Detroit Lions, he was All-NFL HB, served in Navy in World War II. Then he quit pro game and went to Yale law school. ● ●

Today Byron White is one of football's greatest "graduates," as Justice of United States Supreme Court. ●

The 1939 season featured most-inspirational player of the decade: Nile Kinnick, Iowa star of 1937-38-39, who was easily greatest "Iron-Man" in modern history.

SOMEBODY TELL ME HOW THAT KID DOES IT...!

A running, passing, punting, drop-kicking virtuoso, the 5-10, 175-pound tailback played 402 of possible 420 minutes in 1939, went the full 60 in six straight vs. Indiana, Michigan, Wisconsin, Purdue, Notre Dame, Minnesota; was personally involved in 107 of the Hawkeyes' 135 points that year.

He passed for two TDs in fourth period to beat Minnesota; ran for winning TD vs. Notre Dame, climaxed season by winning Heisman, Maxwell and Camp awards, beat out super-star Joe DiMaggio of Yankees as No. 1 athlete-of-year. Like Whizzer White before him, he was also a Phi Beta Kappa scholar.

But fate deserted him as fighter pilot aboard aircraft carrier in World War II. He died in crash at sea. ● ●

In the year just before World War II, Michigan's 6-foot, 195-pound HB, Tom Harmon, was the super-star of football. As prepper in Gary, Ind., he'd been 14-letterman in four sports. Teaming up with QB Forest Evashevski in 1938-39-40, Harmon brought Wolverines out of a long grid drought.

A tremendous runner, passer and kicker, Harmon broke Red Grange's Big Ten scoring record, 33 TDs to 31. Tailback in single-wing, he twice tallied four TDs a game, vs. California and Iowa. Most of his scores came on long, slashing runs.

In three years Harmon carried 398 times for 2338 yards (just under 6 yards per carry); completed 101 of 233 passes (16 TDs); scored 237 points on 33 TDs, PATs and field goals.

All-America in 1939-40, Harmon was Heisman Trophy winner as senior, as well as Associated Press Athlete-of-the-Year. He went into Air Force in World War II. Twice he had to bail out of crippled planes and was given up for lost. Once he came out of jungle a week later; other time he made it back to American base in China after 32 days of hiding from Japs.

The biggest transformation in modern football got its impetus in 1940 from Clark Shaughnessy, who'd replaced Amos Alonzo Stagg at Chicago in 1933, and left for Stanford when the Maroon dropped football after the '39 season was finished.

An ex-Minnesota star who'd never even played in high school, Shaughnessy took with him an idea that would change the game. The year before, Stanford had lost every Conference game. Shaughnessy gave his green team something he'd experimented with while acting as advisor to Chicago Bears.

It was called the T-formation, and directing it for Stanford was a left-handed QB named Frank Albert. ●

One of the great all-time backfields of Albert, HBs Pete Kmetovic and Hugh Gallarneau, and FB Norm Standlee, paced Cinderella Stanford to unbeaten season and Rose Bowl win over Nebraska. After that the T-formation was the thing. ●

The 1940s posed player problems as nation went into World War II. Certain colleges were allowed to use naval trainees on campus. (Army trainees were not allowed to play.) Other schools were limited to a sprinkling of boys unfit for military duty for varied reasons, plus 18-year-old frosh eligible for varsity under war-time rules, but not yet called up by draft. Within this chaotic framework, three great West Point teams, not affected by draft (1944-45-46), dominated the collegiate grid picture.

Cadets went 27 straight without loss in those three years, scoring awesome 1179 points from Coach Earl (Red) Blaik's T-formation, still somewhat new in football. The '44 club set a modern scoring mark of 504 points in only nine games.

It was hard to peg greatness of '44 team because of sub-par foes, but HB Glenn Davis and FB Felix (Doc) Blanchard led contingent of six All-Americas on a team not only explosive offensively but so alert it intercepted record 37 passes. ●

But above all, these Army teams were marked by "Mr. Outside," and "Mr. Inside," whose exploits deserve added emphasis . . . ●●

HB Glenn Davis, "Mr. Outside," for Army, was 5-11, 175-pounder from California. In 1944 he raced for 20 TDs, half of them on runs of 40 yards or more, for modern scoring mark; averaged sensational 11.1 yards per carry. He had blazing speed and a tricky change of pace. In 1945 he scored five TDs against Navy; six TDs vs. Penn. Later Davis was star for Los Angeles Rams. ● ●

FB Felix (Doc) Blanchard, a 6-1, 205-pound South Carolinian, was Cadets' "Mr. Inside." A crunching, powerful line-blaster, he kept opposing defenses honest for Davis' outside forays, yet was fast enough, himself, to sweep the ends. He was also a tremendous blocker, kicker, and devastating as a line-backer. He made service a career and today is an Air Force Colonel.

Despite Glenn Davis' heroics in 1944, Heisman Trophy went to Ohio State QB and dental student Les Horvath, who paced 18-year-old frosh backfield mates, led Buckeyes to unbeaten season with his running, passing and play-calling. ● ● ●

Subsequently, Doc Blanchard won Heisman Award in '45; Glenn Davis in '46. In three years (1944-45-46) 10 Army men racked up 16 All-America positions. ● ●

Cadets, unbeaten in three years, finally were brought back to human level in '46 by great Notre Dame team led by QB Johnny Lujack, in titanic 0-0 tie. Lujack would turn out to be undoubtedly the best of all-time modern Irish QBs. ● ● ●

. . . And Notre Dame, under Frank Leahy, after many years since the death of Knute Rockne, was now headed for its second era of collegiate grid greatness.

Frank Leahy, a tackle for Knute Rockne, took coaching reins at Notre Dame in 1941 after success at Boston College and previously as Fordham's line coach where he molded famed "Seven Blocks of Granite." After three years with Irish he went into Navy during war, came back in '46 to establish super-era of Irish football. Before retirement at end of '53 season he would, post gaudiest mark of any modern coach; 87 wins, 11 losses, nine ties.

Inexhaustible perfectionist, Leahy worked til midnight virtually every day of year. He made alumni scream by junking famed Rockne system, developed version of George Halas' T-attack. Methods, personality prompted some to call him "The Master," often in sarcasm—but he kept winning. ● ●

In 1946-47-49 Irish were nation champs; second in '48; undefeated in 38 games. In 1946-47 ND was led by incomparable QB Johnny Lujack, twice All-America, who completed 55% of passes.

In 1947, 6-5, 250-pound end, Leon Hart (who had starred as frosh previous year) made All-America as soph, was one of five Notre Dame choices. He repeated '48-49.

Terry Brennan and Emil "Six-Yards" Sitko, led '48 Irish who gained 3194 yards rushing. ND's 29-game win streak was halted by tie with USC, but Glory Days were not yet finished . . .

In 1949 Notre Dame, trampling 10 foes with 360 points, gave Frank Leahy fifth unbeaten season in seven years. Bob Williams was his third All-America QB (following Angelo Bertelli and John Lujack). Finally, in second game of 1950, Irish streak of 30 without defeat was ended by Purdue, 28-14. In his 11 years Leahy turned out 22 All-Americas. He was only 45 when intensity of coaching pressures got to him.

In 1953 during Georgia Tech game, midway in season that would be his sixth unbeaten, Leahy collapsed of pancreatic attack in locker room between halves, retired at year's end.

Meanwhile, vieing for national honors with Leahy was Michigan's brilliant Orrin (Fritz) Crisler. Crisler, star end for Stagg at Chicago, had been successful at Minnesota and Princeton before Michigan called him in '38 to revive Wolves

IT MIGHT WORK...IT'S WORTH A TRY...!

His Princeton Tigers of 1933-35 had won 25, lost one, were among nation's best. Wolverines had suffered four losing seasons before his arrival. He made them winners. Now, in late 1940s, he came up with idea that quickly changed football . . .

It was Michigan's Fritz Crisler who developed idea of two-platoon football in 1946, taking advantage of unlimited substitution rule put into effect during war. Facing mighty Army with youthful team, Crisler decided to stretch his strength by playing best offensive men when he had ball, best defenders on defense. Wolverines gave Cadets terrific battle before losing but the idea caught on all over nation. Hallmark of Crisler's great teams of late 1940s was buck-lateral and spin-buck single-wing attack.

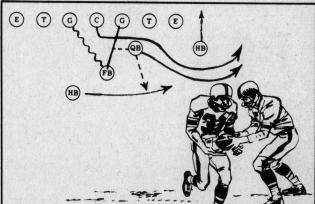

In buck-lateral, FB, instead of blasting into line, sometimes would hand off to QB before going in; QB would pitch lateral to HB going wide—or pass. Defense didn't know which was coming. On spin-buck, the close man would receive snap, spin to give to man coming across. Often he'd fake, complete his spin and in same movement smash back into the line.

Wolves' '47 team featured All-America tailback Bob Chappuis; the Elliot brothers, Bump and Pete; and Tackle Alvin Wistert. After unbeaten, 345-point season in nine games, Wolverines were second to Notre Dame in final national poll. Then came an unprecedented bit of spontaneous business...

After Michigan crushed USC in Rose Bowl, 49-0, fans protested the final balloting, demanded a post-season poll. The Associated Press faced a decision...

In response to fans' clamor, the AP took unprecedented action after Michigan crushed USC in Rose Bowl, held a post-season poll, and Wolverines unofficially replaced Notre Dame as 1947 national champs. It was a fitting swan song for Fritz Crisler who announced retirement as coach, to be succeeded by top aide, Bennie Oosterbaan, with Crisler remaining as Athletic Director. But Michigan's re-emergence as national power had not yet run its course...

In 1948, Wolverines swept to another unbeaten season, left no doubt this time who was No. 1. One big reason was Alvin Wistert, who completed a Michigan trilogy unique in grid history: he was third Wistert to be named All-America tackle, following his older brothers Francis, '33; Albert '42. ● ● ●

Bennie Oosterbaan also helped make history when he succeeded Crisler as Coach-of-the-Year, the only time a college had produced two straight winners of award.

One of decade's most glamorous stars was Southern Methodist's Doak Walker, 175-pound, picture-book QB who ran and passed his way to fame as only back in Southwest Conference annals on three straight All-Americas, 1947-48-49. ● ● ●

Football in the Fifties was marked by rise of Oklahoma as awesome national power. The Sooners were led by Charles (Bud) Wilkinson, ex-Minnesota star, who, taking over in 1947, soon established himself as one of game's great coaches. ● ●

Oklahoma's style was free-wheeling both on offense and defense. From his split-T, Wilkinson made virtually every wide running play, every pass play an option. He also drilled hard-nosed defense to quickly realign after snap to meet the play.

Lean, fast players were Oklahoma trademark. They sprinted out of huddle. Sooners were undefeated in 1950-54-55-56, were National Champs in 50-55-56. The '56 team set modern scoring record of 466 points. At retirement after 1963 season, Wilkinson left a spectacular 145-29-4 coaching mark, and a record 23 All-America players by one coach. Later, he went into politics. ● ● ●

In 1950-51 Princeton, under Charles Caldwell, the last major disciple of the single wing, fielded the best back-to-back teams the East had seen in years—and, quite possibly, two of best anytime.

Spearhead of the attack which tallied 659 points in two years, was tremendously versatile 175-pound tailback, Dick Kazmaier, a hard, slashing runner and deadly passer who was constant threat on Tigers' potent option sweeps. ●●●

A two-time All-America, Kazmaier was Heisman winner in '50 as he led nation in total offense (1827 yards rushing & passing), the first Easterner ever to win combined yardage crown.

He scored nine TDs, passed for 13 more, had phenomenal aerial completion average of 62.6, and career mark of 35 TD passes, 4357 total yards.

The 1953 season featured two major developments: (1) Unlimited substitution was thrown out and players again had to go both ways; (2) Gen. Robert R. Neyland was now absent from coaching ranks.

Neyland had been star end at West Point; he was also a pitcher who won 20 straight, and cadet heavyweight boxing king. In 1926, as a Captain, he was assigned to teach military tactics at Tennessee—and also wound up as Vols' grid coach.

Between tours of Army duty, Neyland had three hitches at Tennessee, 1926-34; 36-40; 46-52. In 21 seasons he was the winningest coach in Southern annals with a brilliant 173-31-12 mark. Eight clubs were unbeaten (1927-28-29-31-32-38-39-40), a major college coaching record.

All-time defensive leader, Neyland held foes scoreless in 110 of 173 wins; lifetime, held them under 5 points per game. Stars and future coaches galore got their skills under him: Gene McEver, Bobby Dodd, Beattie Feathers, Herman Hickman, Bowden Wyatt, Murray Warmath, among others. ● ●

Coming on as big coaching success in mid-Fifties was Ohio State's Woody Hayes whose 1954-55-57 clubs were Big Ten titlists and '54, '57 (and later '68) teams were selected as national champs.

Buckeyes displayed tremendous ball-control ground game, passing just enough to vary attack. Also featured in '54-'55 was the sensational running and all-around pyrotechnics of 178-pound HB, Howard (Hopalong) Cassady, two-time All-America and an overwhelming Heisman choice in 1955.

One of the most dramatic sequences of the decade came in the Buckeyes' '54 finale with Michigan, with Rose Bowl bid at stake. With game tied, Wolverines had first down on Ohio State's four-yard line—were stopped four plays later one foot from goal line. Then, with Cassady leading the drive, the Buckeyes went 99⅔ yards for the winning touchdown and a ticket to Pasadena.

In 1957 the longest winning streak in modern football history was broken when Notre Dame tallied the game's only TD for 7-0 victory, over Oklahoma, ending Sooners' string at 47.

In 1958, college rules makers dramatically announced football's first change in scoring system unaltered in 46 years.

THEY'VE GOT GUTS! GOING FOR TWO INSTEAD OF THE TIE!

From now on, teams had the option of kicking for a one-pointer on the PAT, or running or passing for two points. Fans liked this extra dimension of excitement and strategy. ●●

The next year, goal posts were widened from 18½ feet to 23 feet 4 inches, a more tempting shot for strategists and field goal kickers. ●●

The 1960s brought no significant rules changes, although, in 1964, due to pressures from coaches, the rules committee restored what was virtually unlimited substitution and two-platoon football. Essentially, the decade produced glamorous coaches and the rise of pro game to spectacular heights of fan appeal.

Paul Bryant, after brief coaching stints at Maryland, Kentucky and Texas A. & M., came home in 1958 to Alabama where he'd been a star end in 1934. 'Bama was in the gridiron doldrums, but not for long, as Bryant turned things around. ● ● ●

A persuasive recruiter and tough drill-master, Bryant quickly had the Crimson Tide rolling again. Like Wilkinson at Oklahoma, he preferred players lean and fast, including linemen, took them to 10 Bowl games in 10 years for a Bowl record.

Bright star of Bryant's 1962-63-64 clubs was Joe Namath, a tough, lanky passing whiz at QB whose fame would soon escalate in pro ranks.

By the mid-1960s, Michigan State's Hugh (Duffy) Daugherty was established as an all-time coaching great. Daugherty succeeded Biggie Munn in 1954 after Munn retired from great career to be full-time Athletic Director.

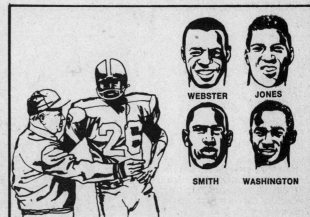

WEBSTER   JONES

SMITH   WASHINGTON

Daugherty was not only one of game's great humorists but a brilliant architect of a multi-faceted T-attack. His undefeated Big Ten champs in 1965-66 were among greatest of modern teams (although '65 club was upset by UCLA in Rose Bowl).

The '65 Spartans set an all-time record by placing seven men on the All-America squads, and five more in '66 for still another record two-year total. In '66 with the national championship at stake in one of most heralded games in history, unbeaten MSU and unbeaten Notre Dame played an epic 10-10 tie, with Irish criticized for running out the clock in final minute to preserve the deadlock.

Another glamor coach of 1960s was Notre Dame's Ara Parseghian, who arrived at South Bend in 1963, immediately established the Era of Ara in restoring Irish as national power after several lacklustre years.

Parseghian was a product of Miami of Ohio, incubator of amazing number of great coaches, including Red Blaik, Paul Brown, Woody Hayes, Sid Gillman, Weeb Ewbank, John Pont. A halfback, he played for Cleveland Browns before coaching.

A Protestant of Armenian descent at a Catholic School, Parseghian was immensely popular with students and alumni.

John McKay, of Southern California, restored the Trojans to the great heights they knew in the 1920s and 1930s under fabled Howard Jones.

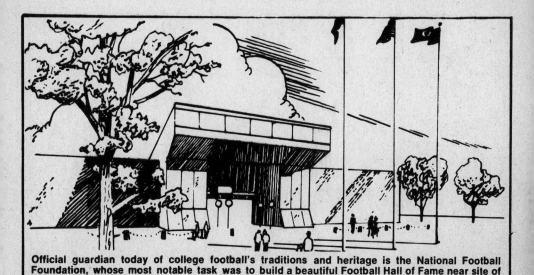

Official guardian today of college football's traditions and heritage is the National Football Foundation, whose most notable task was to build a beautiful Football Hall of Fame near site of the historic first game between Rutgers and Princeton on that eventful Nov. 6, 1869. ● ● ●

The striking edifice will be the repository for nation's greatest collection of records, historic films, pictures, and other grid memorabilia.

Alumni and fans will be able to push a button and see and hear vital facts about their school's educational and football background. Companion shrine to Collegiate Hall of Fame is Pro Football's Hall at Canton, O. (Next: Pro Football.) ●

YOU'VE GOT THE EXPERIENCE WE NEED, JOHN!

In August of 1895, John Brailler, a Latrobe, Pa., dentist, and former college player, had been recruited by town football team to play QB against arch-rival from nearby Jeannette. Offered $10, it was first anyone had been paid for playing.

It wasn't long before town teams in Western Pennsylvania were luring ex-collegians with the same tactics.

GEE, THAT'S JIM THORPE!

But pro football, in an organized way, got its real start in Canton and Massillon, O., where pay-for-play by 1905 was being formed on a town league basis. Soon there were several formal teams all over Ohio. Bidding for players was fierce.

Known as the Canton Bulldogs and Massillon Tigers, these two clubs led the way in recruiting such ex-collegians as Jim Thorpe, Knute Rockne, Willie Heston, and Pudge Heffelfinger. ●●●

Pro football's big step forward was taken at Canton, O., in 1920 with formation of American Professional Football Assn. Teams were from Canton, Massillon, Cleveland, Akron, Dayton, Rochester, N. Y., Decatur, Ill., Rock Island, Ill., Muncie, Ind. and Hammond, Ind. Many, of course, were small cities.

League's first president was Jim Thorpe but he wasn't strong administrator and in 1921 Joe Carr, of Columbus, O., was named president and took firm command by insisting that the loosely-run group adopt two basic building rules: teams had to honor contracts of players signed by other teams, and could not sign players with college eligibility remaining. In 1922 the organization was re-named the National Football League.

One of pioneer pro leaders was young George Halas, fresh out of Illinois, who in 1922 took the Decatur franchise to Chicago, re-named the team The Bears. Franchises in that day could be bought for a mere $100.

In same year young Curly Lambeau got a local meat packer to back a team in a small Wisconsin city, to be called the Green Bay Packers. Lambeau and Halas, supreme optimists of early pro days, helped Carr nurse the impossible dream.

It didn't seem that pro ball would survive in the 1920s as teams formed and folded all over the East and Midwest in such places as Frankford, Pa.; Portsmouth, O.; Racine, Wisc.; Pottsville, Pa.; Duluth, Minn. The public was unimpressed.

In 1925 two things helped save pro ball. Tim Mara, a New York race track bookie, bought a franchise for an astronomical $2500 — and Red Grange, leaving Illinois at season's end, signed with the Chicago Bears. Publicity from New York and Grange's magic name started drawing fans. In his first appearance as pro, Grange drew 36,000 in Chicago. A week later there were 68,000 in New York (Normal attendance for the next 10 years would be a fraction of that, but seeds of interest were planted.) ●● ●

The pros knew the public could be lured only by the signing of big college stars. In 1930 Bronko Nagurski came in; the college boys began to believe there might be some money in this — particularly with minimums and a standard contract.

In 1933 the NFL split into two divisions with a playoff to decide the pro title. The Bears, Packers, and Chicago Cardinals were the only original teams left in the 10-team league. Now, the NFL was only one progressive idea away from success . . .

In 1935, spurred by Bert Bell, President of the Philadelphia Eagles, and later League Commissioner, the pros cleared the way for permanent success by putting in the college draft. This set up an orderly and equitable system of signing talent, guaranteeing a fair method of distributing player strength. It made it impossible for rich clubs to buy up the best players. ●

By World War II, the NFL had produced several super-stars who, for the first time, were vieing for fan attention with the collegians. The Bears were beginning an era of super-team success, led by the "perfect quarterback," Sid Luckman. ●

Luckman, ex-Columbia, was first great T-quarterback, a master tactician, superb passer. The "Monsters", as Bears were called, were unbelievable in swamping Redskins, 73-0, for title in 1940; were in the playoff game four straight seasons.

Meanwhile, Redskins' QB Sammy Baugh, from T.C.U., became legend in his own time, set an all-time pro passing record of 1709 completions (on 3016 attempts) in 16 seasons as a pro, 1937-52.

PAUL BROWN

In 1950, after short-lived All-America Conference folded, Paul Brown, ex-Massillon, O., High School and Ohio State coach, took his Cleveland Browns into the NFL and dominated league, making playoffs six straight years 1950-55, winning three titles.

When Don Hutson, Green Bay Packer end, retired in 1945 after 11 seasons, the ex-Alabama star was noted as greatest receiver in history, his 105 TD passes still an all-time mark.

GRAHAM   GROZA   JIM BROWN

Browns' stars: Otto Graham succeeded Bears' Sid Luckman as Mr. QB, was big threat as a runner as well as deadly passer, devised the now-common clock-killing tactic with minute to play, with short sideline passes. Tackle Lou Groza was game's greatest place-kicker, set all-time scoring mark of 1349 points on 641 PATs, 234 FGs. Fullback Jimmy Brown, on retirement in 1965, was hailed greatest runner of all time. His records: led National Football League rushing 8 times; most yardage rushing lifetime, 12,312; most rushing yardage one season, 1863; and a host of other marks.

The Baltimore Colts who won two straight NFL titles in 1958-59, were clearly one of the greatest pro clubs. Coach Weeb Ewbank in 1956 had turned over the QB job to an unheard of U. of Louisville grad who'd had a trial — and had been released—by Pittsburgh. When the Colts decided to take a chance on him he was getting $6 a game playing sandlot semi-pro ball. When regular QB George Shaw was hurt, he got in. His name: John Unitas. ●●●

The title game in 1958 found the Colts making history by winning first, dramatic, sudden-death overtime playoff, 23-17, vs. Giants, after regulation 17-17 tie; with Alan Ameche plunging for winning TD at 8:15 of overtime period in snowy gloom.

Unitas, from 1956 through next three years, set record by tossing at least one TD pass in 47 straight games. (A year later he broke Sid Luckman's single season record of 28 with 32 TD completions.

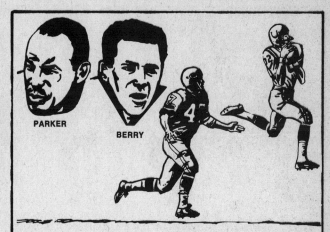

PARKER

BERRY

So deadly was Unitas' arm, the first three Colt receivers in '59, Ray Berry, Lennie Moore and Jim Mutschuller, were 1-2-4 among NFL pass receivers. Much of Unitas' pass protection came from Jim Parker, all-pro tackle, record 8 straight years.

In 1959, an assistant coach of the New York Giants signed on as head man with the Green Bay Packers and a dynasty was born. Vince Lombardi who'd been one of the famed Seven Blocks of Granite at Fordham in the 1930s, had coached in high school, then was assistant coach at Army before joining the Giants. Taking over the Packers he combined toughness, organizational skill and tactical brilliance to dominate the the pro game for many years.

Leading the Packer charge was QB Bart Starr, ex-Alabama, a cool, pin-point passer, short or long, and canny tactician.

Adding color to the Packer picture was Ray Nitschke, who, with N. Y. Giants' Sam Huff, made linebacking spot the most glamorous defensive position in pro ball. ●

LOMBARDI

Winning the NFL title three years in row, 1965-66-67, gave Packers an all-time pro record. At end of '67 season General Mgr. Vince Lombardi turned over coaching duties to Phil Bengtson, but Packer success was an established product.

Pro ball had reached a major turning point in 1960 when the American Football League was formed and, because of TV, was able to survive financially. But the two rival leagues soon found themselves locked in an off-the-field battle that fans found as fascinating as anything on the turf: the battle of the bonuses as college stars got rich as the NFL and AFL competed for their talented services.

The trend was set quickly by bonuses of $50,000 or more but when the New York Jets gave Alabama's Joe Namath a package deal of $400,000 the sky became the limit. Deals soared to a half million and more for 22-year-old collegians. ● ●

The NFL had hoped the AFL would collapse but it didn't. There was only one way left to eliminate the financially disastrous recruiting war: a common draft of college players. It came in 1967. Along with the peace plan came the first Super Bowl between the NFL and AFL champs. The Green Bay Packers swamped the Kansas City Chiefs in this first epic, and football finally had a system producing a true World Champion, something fans had demanded of the two leagues.

As football entered its Centennial year of 1969 it hailed perhaps the greatest college running back of all time—O. J. Simpson, Southern Cal's 6-2, 205-pound, 9.4 power sprinter whose senior year saw him setting modern NCAA marks of 355 carries, 1709 yards gained, 22 TDs. His two-year record (after transferring from San Francisco Junior College) was 626, 3157, 36 respectively. Unfortunately for O. J., the Heisman winner and Everybody's player-of-the-year, a big climax to his college career was denied him...

In the Rose Bowl against Ohio State, Simpson got away on one of his patented, twisting runs of 80 yards for a TD...But the youthful Buckeyes, who started 13 sophs on offense-defense (unheard of in all Bowl history), were picked up by soph Rex Kern, and came roaring back to blast the Trojans, 27-16.

Meanwhile, the Super Bowl game on Jan. 12, 1969, saw the Jets in an astounding upset, manhandle the Colts, 16-7, to win the world championship as QB Joe Namath punctured Baltimore with his passes and FB Matt Snell blasted for big yardage on the ground, for the first AFL triumph over the NFL. More history would be made in 1970 when the two leagues were scheduled to merge into a new, integrated professional set-up with an exciting, fresh concept in playing alignments. ● ●

THE ALL-AMERICA TEAMS

All-America teams have been selected since 1889 when Caspar Whitney launched the idea for *Harper's Weekly*. Walter Camp, considered by many to be the Father of Modern Football, became the fashionable expert in 1897, and it wasn't long before other sports authorities, magazines and newspapers, and press associations got into the act.

Following are the players who were named by any of the dozen or so respected selectors of All-America squads.

1889
ENDS—Amos Alonzo Stagg, Yale; Arthur Cumnock, Harvard
TACKLES—Hector Cowan, Princeton; Charles Gill, Yale
GUARDS—William Heffelfinger, Yale; John Cranston, Harvard
CENTER—William George, Princeton
BACKS—Edgar Allan Poe, Princeton; Roscoe Channing, Princeton; Knowlton Ames, Princeton; James Lee, Harvard

1890
ENDS—Frank Hallowell, Harvard; Ralph Warren, Princeton
TACKLES—Marshall Newell, Harvard; William Rhodes, Yale
GUARDS—William Heffelfinger, Yale; Jesse Riggs, Princeton
CENTER—John Cranston, Harvard
BACKS—Thomas McClung, Yale; Sheppard Homans, Princeton; Dudley Dean, Harvard; John Corbett, Harvard

1891
ENDS—Frank Hinkey, Yale; John Hartwell, Yale
TACKLES—Wallace Winter, Yale; Marshall Newell, Harvard
GUARDS—William Heffelfinger, Yale; Jesse Riggs, Princeton
CENTER—John Adams, Pennsylvania
BACKS—Philip King, Princeton; Everett Lake, Harvard; Thomas McClung, Yale; Sheppard Homans, Princeton

1892
ENDS—Frank Hinkey, Yale; Frank Hallowell, Harvard
TACKLES—Marshall Newell, Harvard; A. Hamilton Wallis, Yale
GUARDS—Arthur Wheeler, Princeton; Bertram Waters, Harvard
CENTER—William Lewis, Harvard
BACKS—Charles Brewer, Harvard; Vance McCormick, Yale; Philip King, Princeton; Harry Thayer, Pennsylvania

1893
ENDS—Frank Hinkey, Yale; Thomas Trenchard, Princeton
TACKLES—Langdon Lea, Princeton; Marshall Newell, Harvard
GUARDS—Arthur Wheeler, Princeton; William Hickok, Yale
CENTER—William Lewis, Harvard
BACKS—Philip King, Princeton; Charles Brewer, Harvard; Franklin Morse, Princeton; Frank Butterworth, Yale

1894
ENDS—Frank Hinkey, Yale; Charles Gelbert, Pennsylvania
TACKLES—Bertram Waters, Harvard; Langdon Lea, Princeton
GUARDS—Arthur Wheeler, Princeton; William Hickok, Yale
CENTER—Philip Stillman, Yale
BACKS—George Adee, Yale; Arthur Knipe, Pennsylvania; George Brooke, Pennsylvania; Frank Butterworth, Yale

1895
ENDS—Norman Cabot, Harvard; Charles Gelbert, Pennsylvania
TACKLES—Langdon Lea, Princeton; Fred Murphy, Yale
GUARDS—Charles Wharton, Pennsylvania; Dudley Riggs, Princeton
CENTER—Alfred Bull, Pennsylvania
BACKS—Clinton Wyckoff, Cornell; Samuel Thorne, Yale; Arthur Brewer, Harvard; George Brookes, Pennsylvania

1896
ENDS—Norman Cabot, Harvard; Charles Gelbert, Pennsylvania
TACKLES—William Church, Princeton; Fred Murphy, Yale
GUARDS—Charles Wharton, Pennsylvania; Wylie Woodruff, Pennsylvania

CENTER—Robert Gailey, Princeton
BACKS—Clarence Fincke, Yale; Edgar Wrightington, Harvard; Addison Kelly, Princeton; John Baird, Princeton

1897

ENDS—Garrett Cochran, Princeton; John A. Hall, Yale
TACKLES—Burr C. Chamberlin, Yale; John Outland, Pennsylvania
GUARDS—T. Truxtun Hare, Pennsylvania; Gordon Brown, Yale
CENTER—Alan Doucette, Harvard
BACKS—Charles DeSaulles, Yale; Benjamin Dibblee, Harvard; Addison Kelly, Princeton; John Minds, Pennsylvania

1898

ENDS—Lew Palmer, Princeton; John Hallowell, Harvard
TACKLES—Arthur Hillebrand, Princeton; Burr C. Chamberlin, Yale
GUARDS—T. Truxtun Hare, Pennsylvania; Gordon Brown, Yale; Walter Boal, Harvard
CENTERS—Pete Overfield, Pennsylvania; William Cunningham, Michigan
BACKS—Charles Daly, Harvard; Benjamin Dibblee, Harvard; John Outland, Pennsylvania; Clarence Herschberger, Chicago; Malcolm McBride, Yale; Charles Romeyn, Army

1899

ENDS—David Campbell, Harvard; Arthur Poe, Princeton;
TACKLES—Arthur Hillebrand, Princeton; George Stillman, Yale
GUARDS—T. Truxtun Hare, Pennsylvania; Gordon Brown, Yale
CENTER—Pete Overfield, Pennsylvania
BACKS—Charles Daly, Harvard; Josiah McCracken, Pennsylvania; Malcolm McBride, Yale; Isaac Seneca, Carlisle; Albert Sharpe, Yale; Howard Reiter, Princeton

1900

ENDS—John Hallowell, Harvard; David Campbell, Harvard; William Smith, Army
TACKLES—George Stillman, Yale; James Bloomer, Yale
GUARDS—Gordon Brown, Yale; T. Truxtun Hare, Pennsylvania
CENTERS—Herman Olcott, Yale; W. E. Bachman, Lafayette
BACKS—Bill Morley, Columbia; George Chadwick, Yale; Perry Hale, Yale; William Fincke, Yale; Charles Daly, Harvard; Raymond Starbuck, Cornell

1901

ENDS—David Campbell, Harvard; Ralph Davis, Princeton; Edward Bowditch, Harvard; Neil Snow, Michigan
TACKLES—Oliver Cutts, Harvard; Paul Bunker, Army; Crawford Blagden, Harvard
GUARDS—William Warner, Cornell; William Lee, Harvard; Charles Barnard, Harvard; Sanford Hunt, Cornell
CENTERS—Henry Holt, Yale; W. E. Bachman, Lafayette
BACKS—Robert Kernan, Harvard; Charles Daly, Army; Thomas Graydon, Harvard; Harold Weekes, Columbia; Bill Morley, Columbia

1902

ENDS—Thomas Shevlin, Yale; Edward Bowditch, Harvard
TACKLES—Ralph Kinney, Yale; James Hogan, Yale; Paul Bunker, Army
GUARDS—Edgar Glass, Yale; John DeWitt, Princeton; William Warner, Cornell
CENTERS—Henry Holt, Yale; Robert Boyers, Army
BACKS—Foster Rockwell, Yale; George Chadwick, Yale; Thomas Graydon, Harvard; Paul Bunker, Army; T. A. Barry, Brown

1903

ENDS—Howard Henry, Princeton; Charles Rafferty, Yale
TACKLES—Daniel Knowlton, Harvard; James Hogan, Yale; Fred Schacht, Minnesota
GUARDS—John DeWitt, Princeton; Andrew Marshall, Harvard; James Bloomer, Yale
CENTER—Henry Hooper, Dartmouth
BACKS—Willie Heston, Michigan; J. Dana Kafer, Princeton; James Johnson, Carlisle; Richard Smith, Columbia; Myron Witham, Dartmouth; W. Ledyard Mitchell, Yale

1904

ENDS—Thomas Shevlin, Yale; F. A. Speik, Chicago
TACKLES—James Hogan, Yale; James Cooney, Princeton
GUARDS—Frank Piekarski, Pennsylvania; Joseph Gilman, Dartmouth; Ralph Kinney, Yale
CENTER—Arthur Tipton, Army
BACKS—Daniel Hurley, Harvard; Walter Eckersall, Chicago; Vincent Stevenson, Pennsylvania; Willie Heston, Michigan; Andrew Smith, Pennsylvania; Foster Rockwell, Yale; Henry Torney, Army

1905

ENDS—Thomas Shevlin, Yale; Ralph Glaze, Dartmouth; Mark Catlin, Chicago
TACKLES—Otis Lamson, Pennsylvania; Beaton Squires, Harvard; Karl Brill, Harvard
GUARDS—Roswell Tripp, Yale; Francis Burr, Harvard
CENTER—Robert Torrey, Pennsylvania
BACKS—Walter Eckersall, Chicago; Howard Roome, Yale; John Hubbard, Amherst; James McCormick, Princeton; Guy Hutchinson, Yale; Daniel Hurley, Harvard; Henry Torney, Army

1906

ENDS—L. Casper Wister, Princeton; Robert Forbes, Yale
TACKLES—L. Horatio Biglow, Yale; James Cooney, Princeton; Charles Osborne, Harvard
GUARDS—Francis Burr, Harvard; Elmer Thompson, Cornell; August Ziegler, Pennsylvania
CENTERS—William T. Dunn, Penn State; William Newman, Cornell
BACKS—Walter Eckersall, Chicago; Hugh Knox, Yale; John Mayhew, Brown; Paul Veeder, Yale; Edward Dillon, Princeton; William Hollenback, Pennsylvania

1907

ENDS—Clarence Alcott, Yale; Bill Dague, Navy; Albert A. Exendine, Carlisle; L. Casper Wister, Princeton
TACKLES—Dexter Draper, Pennsylvania; L. Horatio Biglow, Yale
GUARDS—August Ziegler, Pennsylvania; William Erwin, Army
CENTERS—Adolph Schulz, Michigan; Patrick Grant, Harvard
BACKS—Thomas A. D. Jones, Yale; John Wendell, Harvard; Edwin Harlan, Princeton; James McCormick, Princeton; Edward Coy, Yale; Peter Hauser, Carlisle

1908

ENDS—Hunter Scarlett, Pennsylvania; George Schildmiller, Dartmouth
TACKLES—Hamilton Fish, Harvard; M. Frank Horr, Syracuse; Percy Northcroft, Navy
GUARDS—William Goebel, Yale; Clark Tobin, Dartmouth; Hamlin Andrus, Yale; Bernard O'Rourke, Cornell
CENTER—Charles Nourse, Harvard
BACKS—William Hollenback, Pennsylvania; Frederick Tibbott, Princeton; Edward Coy, Yale; Walter Steffen, Chicago; Ed Lange, Navy; Hamilton Corbett, Harvard

1909

ENDS—John Reed Kilpatrick, Yale; Adrian Regnier, Brown
TACKLES—Hamilton Fish, Harvard; Henry Hobbs, Yale
GUARDS—Albert Benbrook, Michigan; Hamlin Andrus, Yale
CENTER—Carroll Cooney, Yale
BACKS—Edward Coy, Yale; John McGovern, Minnesota; Stephen Philbin, Yale; Wayland Minot, Harvard

1910

ENDS—John Reed Kilpatrick, Yale; Stanfield Wells, Michigan
TACKLES—Robert McKay, Harvard; James Walker, Minnesota
GUARDS—Robert Fisher, Harvard; Albert Benbrook, Michigan
CENTER—Ernest Cozens, Pennsylvania
BACKS—E. LeRoy Mercer, Pennsylvania; Percy Wendell, Harvard; W. Earl Sprackling, Brown; Talbot Pendleton, Princeton

1911

ENDS—Douglass Bomeisler, Yale; Sanford White, Princeton
TACKLES—Edward Hart, Princeton; Leland Devore, Army
GUARDS—Robert Fisher, Harvard; Joseph Duff, Princeton
CENTER—Henry Ketcham, Yale
BACKS—Jim Thorpe, Carlisle; Percy Wendell, Harvard; Arthur Howe, Yale; Jack Dalton, Navy

1912

ENDS—Samuel Felton, Harvard; Douglass Bomeisler, Yale
TACKLES—Wesley Englehorn, Dartmouth; Robert Butler, Wisconsin
GUARDS—Stanley Pennock, Harvard; W. John Logan, Princeton
CENTER—Henry Ketcham, Yale
BACKS—Charles Brickley, Harvard; Jim Thorpe, Carlisle; George Crowther, Brown; E. LeRoy Mercer, Pennsylvania

1913

ENDS—Robert Hogsett, Dartmouth; Louis Merillat, Army
TACKLES—Harold Ballin, Princeton; Nelson Talbott, Yale; Miller Pontius, Michigan; Harvey R. Hitchcock, Harvard
GUARDS—John Brown, Navy; Stanley Pennock, Harvard; Ray Keeler, Wisconsin
CENTER—Paul Des Jardien, Chicago
BACKS—Charles Brickley, Harvard; Edward Mahan, Harvard; James Craig, Michigan; Ellery Huntington, Colgate; Charles Dorais, Notre Dame

1914

ENDS—Huntington Hardwick, Harvard; John O'Hearn, Cornell; Perry Graves, Illinois
TACKLES—Harold Ballin, Princeton; Walter Trumbull, Harvard; Vic Halligan, Nebraska
GUARDS—Stanley Pennock, Harvard; Ralph Chapman, Illinois; Arlie Mucks, Wisconsin; Clarence Spears, Dartmouth
CENTERS—John McEwan, Army; Robert Peck, Pittsburgh
BACKS—John Maulbetsch, Michigan; Milton Ghee, Dartmouth; Frederick Bradlee, Harvard; Edward Mahan, Harvard; Charles Barrett, Cornell; John E. Spiegel, Washington & Jefferson; Harry Legore, Yale

1915

ENDS—Bert Baston, Minnesota; Murray Shelton, Cornell; Guy Chamberlin, Nebraska; Bob Higgins, Penn State
TACKLES—Joseph Gilman, Harvard; Earl Abell, Colgate; Howard Buck, Wisconsin; M. M. Witherspoon, Washington & Jefferson
GUARDS—Clarence Spears, Dartmouth; Christopher Schlachter, Syracuse; Harold A. White, Syracuse
CENTER—Robert Peck, Pittsburgh
BACKS—Charles Barrett, Cornell; Edward Mahan, Harvard; Richard King, Harvard; Bart Macomber, Illinois; Eugene Mayer, Virginia; Neno Jerry DePrato, Michigan State

1916

ENDS—Bert Baston, Minnesota; George Moseley, Yale; James Herron, Pittsburgh
TACKLES—Clarence Horning, Colgate; D. Belford West, Colgate; Robert Karch, Ohio State
GUARDS—Clinton Black, Yale; Harrie Dadmun, Harvard; Frank Hogg, Princeton
CENTER—Robert Peck, Pittsburgh
BACKS—Elmer Oliphant, Army; Fritz Pollard, Brown; Oscar Anderson, Colgate; Charles Harley, Ohio State; Claire Long, Minnesota; Stan Cofall, Notre Dame

1917

ENDS—Charles Bolen, Ohio State; Paul Robeson, Rutgers
TACKLES—Wilbur Henry, Washington & Jefferson; Walker Carpenter, Georgia Tech
GUARDS—Frank Culver, Michigan; C. G. Higgins, Chicago
CENTER—Russell Bailey, West Virginia
BACKS—George Strupper, Georgia Tech; Elmer Oliphant, Army; George McLaren, Pittsburgh; Ben Boynton, Williams

1918

ENDS—Paul Robeson, Rutgers; Robert Hopper, Pennsylvania; Bill Fincher, Georgia Tech
TACKLES—Leonard Hilty, Pittsburgh; Lou Usher, Syracuse; Joe Guyon, Georgia Tech; Wilbur Henry, Washington & Jefferson
GUARDS—Joe Alexander, Syracuse; Lyman Perry, Navy
CENTERS—Ashel Day, Georgia Tech; John Depler, Illinois
BACKS—Frank Murrey, Princeton; Tom Davies, Pittsburgh; Wolcott Roberts, Navy; Frank Steketee, Michigan; George McLaren, Pittsburgh

1919

ENDS—Bob Higgins, Penn State; Henry Miller, Pennsylvania; Lester Belding, Iowa
TACKLES—Wilbur Henry, Washington & Jefferson; D. Belford West, Colgate
GUARDS—Joe Alexander, Syracuse; Adolph Youngstrom, Dartmouth
CENTERS—James Weaver, Centre; Charles Carpenter, Wisconsin
BACKS—Charles Harley, Ohio State; Ira Rodgers, West Virginia; Edward Casey, Harvard; Alvin (Bo) McMillin, Centre; Ben Boynton, Williams

1920

ENDS—Charles Carney, Illinois; Bill Fincher, Georgia Tech; Luke Urban, Boston College; Farnk Weston, Wisconsin
TACKLES—J. Stanton Keck, Princeton; Ralph Scott, Wisconsin; Charles McGuire, Chicago
GUARDS—J. Timothy Callahan, Yale; Thomas Woods, Harvard; James Tolbert, Harvard; Iolas Huffman, Ohio State
CENTER—Herb Stein, Pittsburgh
BACKS—George Gipp, Notre Dame, Gaylord Stinchomb, Ohio State; Charles Way, Penn State; Donald Lourie, Princeton; Ben Boynton, Williams; Tom Davies, Pittsburgh

1921

ENDS—Harold Muller, California; James Roberts, Centre
TACKLES—Russell Stein, Washington & Jefferson; Charles McGuire, Chicago
GUARDS—Frank Schwab, Lafayette; John Brown, Harvard
CENTER—Henry Vick, Michigan
BACKS—Aubrey Devine, Iowa; Edgar Kaw, Cornell; Glenn Killinger, Penn State; Malcolm Aldrich, Yale

1922

ENDS—Harold Muller, California; Wendell Taylor, Navy
TACKLES—C. Herbert Treat, Prineton; John Thurman, Pennsylvania
GUARDS—Frank Schwab, Lafayette; Charles Hubbard, Harvard
CENTER—Edgar Garbisch, Army
BACKS—Harry Kipke, Michigan; Gordon Locke, Iowa; John Thomas, Chicago; Edgar Kaw, Cornell

1923

ENDS—Lynn Bomar, Vanderbilt; Homer Hazel, Rutgers; Heck Wakefield, Vanderbilt; Pete McRae, Syracuse
TACKLES—Century Milstead, Yale; Frank Sundstrom, Cornell; Marty Below, Wisconsin
GUARDS—Charles Hubbard, Harvard; Joe Bedenk, Penn State; James McMillen, Illinois
CENTER—Jack Blott, Michigan
BACKS—Harold (Red) Grange, Illinois; William Mallory, Yale; George Pfann, Cornell; Earl Martineau, Minnesota; Don Miller, Notre Dame

1924

ENDS—Richard Luman, Yale; Henry Bjorkman, Dartmouth; Charles Berry, Lafayette; Heck Wakefield, Vanderbilt; Jim Lawson, Stanford
TACKLES—Ed Weir, Nebraska, Edward McGinley, Pennsylvania
GUARDS—Joseph Pondelik, Chicago; Edgar Garbisch, Army; Edliff Slaughter, Michigan; Carl Diehl, Dartmouth; Gus Farwick, Army
CENTERS—Edwin Horrell, California; Winslow Lovejoy, Yale
BACKS—Harry Stuhldreher, Notre Dame; Harold (Red) Grange, Illinois; Jim Crowley, Notre Dame; Elmer Layden, Notre Dame; Walter Koppisch, Columbia; Homer Hazel, Rutgers

1925

ENDS—Bennie Oosterbaan, Michigan; George Tully, Dartmouth; George Thayer, Pennsylvania; Charles Born, Army
TACKLES—Ed Weir, Nebraska; Ralph Chase, Pittsburgh; Nathan Parker, Dartmouth; Edgar Lindenmeyer, Missouri
GUARDS—Carl Diehl, Dartmouth; Herbert Sturhahn, Yale; Edwin Hess, Ohio State; Brice Taylor, Southern California
CENTERS—Edward McMillan, Princeton; Robert Brown, Michigan
BACKS—Andy Oberlander, Dartmouth; Harold (Red) Grange, Illinois; George Wilson, Washington; Ernie Nevers, Stanford; Benny Friedman, Michigan; Jacob Slagle, Princeton

1926

ENDS—Victor Hanson, Syracuse; Bennie Oosterbaan, Michigan; Hoyt Winslett, Alabama; Ted Shipkey, Stanford; Hal Broda, Brown
TACKLES—Frank Wickhorst, Navy; Orland Smith, Brown; Bud Sprague, Army; Lloyd Yoder, Carnegie Tech; Lon Stiner, Nebraska; Al Lassman, New York U.
GUARDS—Bernie Shively, Illinois; Harry Connaughton, Georgetown; Herbert Sturhahn, Yale; Edwin Hess, Ohio State
CENTERS—Art Boeringer, Notre Dame; John Butler, Pennsylvania
BACKS—Benny Friedman, Michigan; Mort Kaer, Southern California; Herb Joesting, Minnesota; Ralph Baker, Northwestern; Tom Hamilton, Navy; Charles Rodgers, Pennsylvania; Marty Karow, Ohio State; Harry Wilson, Army; Roy Randall, Brown

1927

ENDS—Bennie Oosterbaan, Michigan; Tom Nash, Georgia; Ivey Shiver, Georgia

TACKLES—Jesse Hibbs, Southern California; Ed Hake, Pennsylvania; Bud Sprague, Army; Leo Raskowski, Ohio State; John Smith, Pennsylvania; Sidney Quarrier, Yale

GUARDS—John Smith, Notre Dame; William Webster, Yale; Harold Hanson, Minnesota; Russ Crane, Illinois

CENTERS—Larry Bettencourt, St. Mary's; John Charlesworth, Yale

BACKS—Gilbert Welch, Pittsburgh; Morley Drury, Southern California; Herb Joesting, Minnesota; Chris Cagle, Army; Bill Spears, Vanderbilt; Christy Flanagan, Notre Dame

1928

ENDS—Wesley Fesler, Ohio State; Irv Phillips, California; Ike Frankian, St. Mary's; Dale Vansickle, Florida; Theodore Rosenzweig, Carnegie Tech; Kenneth Haycraft, Minnesota

TACKLES—Otto Pommerening, Michigan; Mike Getto, Pittsburgh; Frank Speer, Georgia Tech; Fred Miller, Notre Dame; Albert Nowack, Illinois

GUARDS—Seraphim Post, Stanford; Ed Burke, Navy; George Gibson, Minnesota; Don Robesky, Stanford; Forrest M. Douds, Washington & Jefferson; Dan McMullen, Nebraska

CENTERS—Peter Pund, Georgia Tech; Charles Howe, Princeton

BACKS—Chris Cagle, Army; Ken Strong, New York U.; Howard Harpster, Carnegie Tech; Chuck Carroll, Washington; Paul Scull, Pennsylvania; Earl Clark, Colorado College; Warner Mizell, Georgia Tech

1929

ENDS—Joe Donchess, Pittsburgh; Francis Tappaan, Southern Caifornia; Wesley Fesler, Ohio State; Wear Schoonover, Arkansas; Robert Tanner, Minnesota

TACKLES—Bronko Nagurski, Minnesota; Elmer Sleight, Purdue; Marion Hammon, Southern Methodist; George Ackerman, St. Mary's

GUARDS—Jack Cannon, Notre Dame; Ray Montgomery, Pittsburgh; Bert Schwartz, California

CENTER—Ben Ticknor, Harvard

BACKS—Frank Carideo, Notre Dame; Ralph Welch, Pudue; Chris Cagle, Army; Toby Uansa, Pittsburgh; Tony Holm, Alabama; Gene McEver, Tennessee; Merle Hufford, Washington; Willis Glassgow, Iowa; Willis Banker, Tulane; Earl Pomeroy, Utah

1930

ENDS—Wesley Fesler, Ohio State; Frank Baker, Northwestern; Jerry Dalrymple, Tulane

TACKLES—Fred Sington, Alabama; A. G. Edwards, Washington State; Milo Lubratovich, Wisconsin; Hugh Rhea, Nebraska; Mel Hein, Washington State

GUARDS—Ted Beckett, California; Bert Metzger, Notre Dame; Wade Woodworth, Northwestern; Henry Wisniewski, Fordham; Ralph Maddox, Georgia; Barton Koch, Baylor; Frederick Linehan, Yale

CENTER—Ben Ticknor, Harvard

BACKS—Frank Carideo, Notre Dame; Len Macaluso, Colgate; Marchy Schwartz, Notre Dame; Erny Pinckert, Southern California; Phil Moffett, Stanford; Jim Murphy, Fordham; Bobby Dodd, Tennessee; Marty Brill, Notre Dame; Fayette (Reb) Russell, Northwestern

1931

ENDS—Jerry Dalrymple, Tulane; Vernon Smith, Georgia; John Orsi, Colgate; Henry Cronkite, Kansas State

TACKLES—Jess Quatse, Pittsburgh; Dallas Marvil, Northwestern; Paul Schwegler, Washington; Joe Kurth, Notre Dame; Jack Price, Army; Jack Riley, Northwestern

GUARDS—Clarence Munn, Minnesota; John Baker, Southern California; Nordy Hoffman, Notre Dame; Herman Hickman, Tennessee

CENTERS—Tommy Yarr, Notre Dame; Charles Miller, Purdue; Maynard Morrison, Michigan

BACKS—Marchy Schwartz, Notre Dame; Pug Rentner, Northwestern; Gus Shaver, Southern California; Barry Wood, Harvard; Jimmy Cain, Alabama; Erny Pinckert, Southern California; Don Zimmerman, Tulane

1932

ENDS—Paul Moss, Purdue; Joe Skladany, Pittsburgh; Jose Martinez-Zorilla, Cornell; Dave Nisbet, Washington; Fred Petoskey, Michigan

TACKLES—Joe Kurth, Notre Dame; Ernie Smith, Southern California

GUARDS—Milt Summerfelt, Army; Bill Corbus, Stanford; Robert Smith, Colgate; John Vaught, Texas Christian; Aaron Rosenberg, Southern California

CENTERS—Lawrence Ely, Nebraska; Pete Gracey, Vanderbilt; Charles Bernard, Michigan; Arthur Krueger, Marquette

BACKS—Harry Newman, Michigan; Warren Heller, Pittsburgh; Jimmy Hitchcock, Auburn; Don Zimmerman, Tulane; Frank Christiensen, Utah; Angel Brovelli, St. Mary's; Roy Horstmann, Purdue

1933

ENDS—Joe Skladany, Pittsburgh; Paul Geisler, Centenary; Edgar Manske, Northwestern; Frank Larson, Minnesota; Bill Smith, Washington; Tony Matal, Columbia

TACKLES—Fred Crawford, Duke; Francis Wistert, Michigan; Charles Ceppi, Princeton; Ade Schwammel, Oregon State

GUARDS—Bill Corbus, Stanford; Aaron Rosenberg, Southern California; Francis Schammel, Iowa; Larry Stevens, Southern California

CENTER—Charles Bernard, Michigan

BACKS—Cotton Warburton, Southern California; George Sauer, Nebraska; Beattie Feathers, Tennessee; Duane Purvis, Purdue; Jack Buckler, Army; Francis Lund, Minnesota; Norman Franklin, Oregon State

1934

ENDS—Don Hutson, Alabama; Frank Larson, Minnesota; Monk Moscrip, Stanford; Merle Wendt, Ohio State
TACKLES—Bill Lee, Alabama; Bob Reynolds, Stanford; James Steen, Syracuse; George Maddox, Kansas State; Clyde Carter, Southern Methodist; Ed Widseth, Minnesota
GUARDS—George Barclay, North Carolina; Bill Bevan, Minnesota; Charles Hartwig, Pittsburgh; Regis Monahan, Ohio State; Ken Ormiston, Pittsburgh
CENTERS—George Shotwell, Pittsburgh; Jack Robinson, Notre Dame; Darrell Lester, Texas Christian
BACKS—Francis Lund, Minnesota; Bobby Grayson, Stanford; Fred Borries, Navy; Dixie Howell, Alabama; Bill Wallace, Rice; Jay Berwanger, Chicago; Arleigh Williams, California

1935

ENDS—Wayne Millner, Notre Dame; Gaynell Tinsley, Louisiana State; Monk Moscrip, Stanford; Bill Shuler, Army
TACKLES—Larry Lutz, California; Dick Smith, Minnesota; Ed Widseth, Minnesota; Truman Spain, Southern Methodist
GUARDS—John Weller, Princeton; Sidney Wagner, Michigan State; Paul Tangora, Northwestern; Inwood Smith, Ohio State; J. C. Wetsel, Southern Methodist; Ed Michaels, Villanova
CENTERS—Gomer Jones, Ohio State; Darrell Lester, Texas Christian
BACKS—Jay Berwanger, Chicago; Bobby Grayson, Stanford; Bobby Wilson, Southern Methodist; Riley Smith, Alabama; Sammy Baugh, Texas Christian; Bill Shakespeare, Notre Dame

1936

ENDS—Larry Kelley, Yale; Gaynell Tinsley, Louisiana State
TACKLES—Ed Widseth, Minnesota; Averell Daniell, Pittsburgh; Frank Kinard, Mississippi
GUARDS—Max Starcevich, Washington; Steve Reid, Northwestern; Joe Routt, Texas A&M; John Lautar, Notre Dame; Bill Glassford, Pittsburgh
CENTERS—Alex Wojciechowicz, Fordham; Mike Basrak, Duquesne; Bob Herwig, California
BACKS—Sam Francis, Nebraska; Sammy Baugh, Texas Christian; Clarence Parker, Duke; Ray Buivid, Marquette; Ed Goddard, Washington State; Clint Frank, Yale; Nello Falaschi, Santa Clara; Kent Ryan, Utah State

1937

ENDS—Chuck Sweeney, Notre Dame; Jerome Holland, Cornell; Ray King, Minnesota; Andy Bershak, North Carolina; Perry Schwartz, California; John Wysocki, Villanova
TACKLES—Ed Franco, Fordham; Tony Matisi, Pittsburgh; Vic Markov, Washington; Frank Kinard, Mississippi; Ed Beinor, Notre Dame
GUARDS—Joe Routt, Texas A&M; Leroy Monsky, Alabama; Vard Stockton, California; Gus Zarnas, Ohio State; Phil Daugherty, Santa Clara

CENTERS—Alex Wojciechowicz, Fordham; Carl Hinkle, Vanderbilt
BACKS—Clint Frank, Yale; Marshall Goldberg, Pittsburgh; Byron White, Colorado; Sam Chapman, California; Corby Davis, Indiana; Joe Kilgrow, Alabama

1938

ENDS—Walter Young, Oklahoma; Bowden Wyatt, Tennessee; Jerome Holland, Cornell; Earl Brown, Notre Dame; Bill Daddio, Pittsburgh; John Wysocki, Villanova
TACKLES—Ed Beinor, Notre Dame; Al Wolff, Santa Clara; Bob Voigts, Northwestern; William McKeever, Cornell
GUARDS—Ralph Heikkinen, Michigan; Edward Bock, Iowa State; Bob Suffridge, Tennessee; Elmer Twedell, Minnesota; Sid Roth, Cornell; Harry Smith, Southern California
CENTERS—Ki Aldrich, Texas Christian; Dan Hill, Duke
BACKS—Davey O'Brien, Texas Christian; Marshall Goldberg, Pittsburgh; Bob MacLeod, Dartmouth; Parker Hall, Mississippi; Vic Bottari, California; Johnny Pingel, Michigan State; Eric Tipton, Duke; Howard Weiss, Wisconsin

1939

ENDS—Esco Sarkkinen, Ohio State; Ken Kavanaugh, Louisiana State; Bud Kerr, Notre Dame; Paul Severin, North Carolina; Harlan Gustafson, Pennsylvania; Frank Ivy, Oklahoma
TACKLES—Nick Drahos, Cornell; Harley McCollum, Tulane; Jim Reeder, Illinois; Harry Stella, Army; Joe Boyd, Texas A&M
GUARDS—Harry Smith, Southern California; Ed Molinski, Tennessee; Bob Suffridge, Tennessee
CENTERS—John Schiechl, Santa Clara; John Haman, Northwestern
BACKS—Tommy Harmon, Michigan; Nile Kinnick, Iowa; John Kimbrough, Texas A&M; George Cafego, Tennessee; Banks McFadden, Clemson; Paul Christman, Missouri

1940

ENDS—Gene Goodreault, Boston College; Dave Rankin, Purdue; Buddy Elrod, Mississippi State; Paul Severin, North Carolina; Ed Frutig, Michigan
TACKLES—Nick Drahos, Cornell; Alf Bauman, Northwestern; Bob Reinhard, California; Urban Odson, Minnesota
GUARDS—Bob Suffridge, Tennessee; Warren Alfson, Nebraska; Marshall Robnett, Texas A&M; Augie Lio, Georgetown
CENTERS—Rudy Mucha, Washington; Chet Gladchuck, Boston College; Ray Frick, Pennsylvania
BACKS—Tommy Harmon, Michigan; John Kimbrough, Texas A&M; Frank Albert, Stanford; George Franck, Minnesota

1941

ENDS—Holt Rast, Alabama; Bob Dove, Notre Dame; Malcolm Kutner, Texas; Dave Schreiner, Wisconsin; John Rokisky, Duquesne
TACKLES—Dick Wildung, Minnesota; Ernie Blandin, Tulane; Bob Reinhard, California; Alf Bauman, Northwestern

GUARDS—Endicott Peabody, Harvard; Ray Frankovich, Washington; Bernie Crimmins, Notre Dame; Ralph Fife, Pittsburgh; Chal Daniel, Texas
CENTERS—Darold Jenkins, Missouri; Vince Banonis, Detroit
BACKS—Bruce Smith, Minnesota; Bob Westfall, Michigan; Frank Albert, Stanford; Frank Sinkwich, Georgia; Bill Dudley, Virginia; Steve Lach, Duke

1942

ENDS—Dave Schreiner, Wisconsin; Bob Dove, Notre Dame; Don Currivan, Boston College; Bob Shaw, Ohio State; Bernard Kuczynski, Pennsylvania
TACKLES—Dick Wildung, Minnesota; Albert Wistert, Michigan; Clyde Johnson, Kentucky; Robin Olds, Army; Derrell Palmer, Texas Christian; Charles Csuri, Ohio State
GUARDS—Chuck Taylor, Stanford; Harvey Hardy, Georgia Tech; Julius Franks, Michigan; Lindell Houston, Ohio State; Alex Agase, Illinois; Gerrard Ramsey, William & Mary
CENTERS—Joe Domnanovich, Alabama; George Moseley, Yale; Fred Naumetz, Boston College
BACKS—Frank Sinkwich, Georgia; Paul Governali, Columbia; Mike Holovak, Boston College; Billy Hillenbrand, Indiana; Glenn Dobbs, Tulsa; Angelo Bertelli, Notre Dame; Roy Gafford, Auburn; Jackie Fellows, Fresno State; Bob Kennedy, Washington State; Pat Harder, Wisconsin

1943

ENDS—Ralph Heywood, Southern California; John Yonakor, Notre Dame; Pete Pihos, Indiana; Joe Parker, Texas; Herb Hein, Northwestern; Bob Gantt, Duke
TACKLES—Jim White, Notre Dame; Don Whitmire, Navy; Merv Pregulman, Michigan; Pat Preston, Duke; Art McCaffray, College of the Pacific
GUARDS—Alex Agase, Purdue; John Steber, Georgia Tech; Pat Filley, Notre Dame; George Brown, Navy; Harold Fischer, Southwestern, Tex.
CENTER—Cas Myslinski, Army
BACKS—Bill Daley, Michigan; Angelo Bertelli, Notre Dame; Creighton Miller, Notre Dame; Bob Odell, Pennsylvania; Otto Graham, Northwestern; Tony Butkovich, Purdue; John Podesto, College of the Pacific

1944

ENDS—Phil Tinsley, Georgia Tech; John Dugger, Ohio State; Paul Walker, Yale; Barney Poole, Army; Hub Bechtol, Texas
TACKLES—Don Whitmire, Navy; John Ferraro, Southern California; Bill Willis, Ohio State
GUARDS—Bill Hackett, Ohio State; Ben Chase, Navy; Joe Stanowicz, Army; Hamilton Nichols, Rice; John Green, Army; Bill Hachten, California; Ellis Jones, Tulsa
CENTERS—John Tavener, Indiana; Tex Warrington, Auburn
BACKS—Les Horvath, Ohio State; Glenn Davis, Army; Felix (Doc) Blanchard, Army; Bom Jenkins, Navy; Bob Fenimore, Oklahoma A&M; Boris Dimancheff, Purdue; Doug Kenna, Army; Jug Girard, Wisconsin; Claude (Buddy) Young, Illinois

1945

ENDS—Dick Duden, Navy; Hub Bechtol, Texas; Max Morris, Northwestern; Bob Ravensberg, Indiana; Henry Foldberg, Army
TACKLES—DeWitt Coulter, Army; George Savitsky, Pennsylvania; Albert Nemetz, Army; Mike Castronis, Georgia; Tom Hughes, Purdue
GUARDS—Warren Amling, Ohio State; John Green, Army; John Mastrangelo, Notre Dame
CENTERS—Vaughn Mancha, Alabama; Dick Scott, Navy
BACKS—Glenn Davis, Army; Felix (Doc) Blanchard, Army; Herman Wedemeyer, St. Mary's; Bob Fenimore, Oklahoma A&M; Harry Gilmer, Alabama

1946

ENDS—Burr Baldwin, UCLA; Hub Bechtol, Texas; Henry Foldberg, Army; Elmer Madar, Michigan
TACKLES—George Connor, Notre Dame; Dick Huffman, Tennessee; Warren Amling, Ohio State; George Savitsky, Pennsylvania
GUARDS—Weldon Humble, Rice; Alex Agase, Illinois; John Mastrangelo, Notre Dame
CENTERS—Paul Duke, Georgia Tech; George Strohmeyer, Notre Dame
BACKS—Johnny Lujack, Notre Dame; Glenn Davis, Army; Felix (Doc) Blanchard, Army; Charley Trippi, Georgia; Arnold Tucker, Army

1947

ENDS—Bill Swiacki, Columbia; Paul Cleary, Southern California; Barney Poole, Mississippi; Leon Hart, Notre Dame
TACKLES—Robert Davis, Georgia Tech; George Connor, Notre Dame; John Ferraro, Southern California; Dick Harris, Texas; Ziggy Czarobski, Notre Dame; George Savitsky, Pennsylvania
GUARDS—Joe Steffy, Army; Bill Fischer, Notre Dame; Steve Suhey, Penn State; Rod Franz, California
CENTERS—Chuck Bednarik, Pennsylvania; Dick Scott, Navy
BACKS—Johnny Lujack, Notre Dame; Bob Chappuis, Michigan; Doak Walker, Southern Methodist; Bobby Layne, Texas; Charley Conerly, Mississippi; Ray Evans, Kansas; Chalmers (Bump) Elliott, Michigan; Tony Minisi, Pennsylvania

1948

ENDS—Dick Rifenburg, Michigan; Leon Hart, Notre Dame; Barney Poole, Mississippi; Sam Tamburo, Penn State; George Brodnax, Georgia Tech; Art Weiner, North Carolina
TACKLES—Leo Nomellini, Minnesota; Alvin Wistert, Michigan; Lauri Niemi, Washington State; Paul Lea, Tulane; Jim Turner, California
GUARDS—Buddy Burris, Oklahoma; Bill Fischer, Notre Dame; William Healy, Georgia Tech; Joe Henry, Army; Rod Franz, California; Marty Wendell, Notre Dame
CENTERS—Chuck Bednarik, Pennsylvania; Alex Sarkisian, Northwestern

BACKS—Doak Walker, Southern Methodist; Charley Justice, North Carolina; Jackie Jensen, California; Clyde Scott, Arkansas; John Rauch, Georgia; Bobby Stuart, Army; Art Murakowski, Northwestern; Stan Heath, Nevada; Norm Van Brocklin, Oregon; Emil Sitko, Notre Dame; Bobby Gage, Clemson; Pete Elliott, Michigan; George Taliaferro, Indiana

1949

ENDS—Leon Hart, Notre Dame; James Williams, Rice; Art Weiner, North Carolina; Jim Owens, Oklahoma

TACKLES—Leo Nomellini, Minnesota; Alvin Wistert, Michigan; Wade Walker, Oklahoma; Jim Martin, Notre Dame; Jim Turner, California; Thurman McGraw, Colorado A&M; Allen Wahl, Michigan

GUARDS—Rod Franz, California; Edward Bagdon, Michigan State; John Schweder, Penn; Bernie Barkouskie, Pittsburgh; Stan West, Oklahoma; Lewis McFadin, Texas

CENTERS—Clayton Tonnemaker, Minnesota; Joe Watson, Rice; Tom Novak, Nebraska

BACKS—Emil Sitko, Notre Dame; Doak Walker, Southern Methodist; Arnold Galiffa, Army; Charley Justice, North Carolina; Bob Williams, Notre Dame; Lynn Chandnois, Michigan State; Eddie Price, Tulane; Eddie LeBaron, College of the Pacific; Darrell Royal, Oklahoma

1950

ENDS—Dan Foldberg, Army; Bill McColl, Stanford; Bucky Curtis, Vanderbilt; Don Stonesifer, Northwestern; Frank Anderson, Oklahoma; Don Menasco, Texas; Jim Doran, Iowa State; Dorne Dibble, Michigan State

TACKLES—Jim Weatherall, Oklahoma; Bob Gain, Kentucky; Al Wahl, Michigan; Holland Donan, Princeton; Al Tate, Illinois; Charles Shira, Army; Al Carapella, Miami, Fla.

GUARDS-LINEBACKERS—Lewis McFadin, Texas; Les Richter, California; Ted Daffer, Tennessee; Bob Ward, Maryland; Bob Momsen, Ohio State; Bill Ciaravino, Lehigh

CENTERS-LINEBACKERS—Irvin Holdash, North Carolina; Redmond Finney, Princeton; Elmer Stout, Army; Donn Moomaw, UCLA; Jerry Goom, Notre Dame; Bob McCullough, Ohio State; Bill Vohaska, Illinois

BACKS—Vic Janowicz, Ohio State; Kyle Rote, Southern Methodist; Leon Heath, Oklahoma; Vito Parilli, Kentucky; Bob Williams, Notre Dame; Bob Reynolds, Nebraska; Everett Grandelius, Michigan State; Dick Kazmaier, Princeton; Ed Withers, Wisconsin; Don Heinrich, Washington; Ed Salem, Alabama; Richard Sprague, Washington; Eddie Talboom, Wyoming; Buddy Jones, Oklahoma; Johnny Bright, Drake

1951

ENDS—Bill McColl, Stanford; Bob Carey, Michigan State; Frank McPhee, Princeton; Pat O'Donahue, Wisconsin; Dewey McConnell, Wyoming; Bill Howton, Rice; Hal Faverty, Wisconsin; Ed Bell, Pennsylvania; Stan Williams, Baylor

TACKLES—Don Coleman, Michigan State; Jim Weatherall, Oklahoma; Bill Pearman, Tennessee; Bob Toneff, Notre

Dame; Charles Ulrich, Illinois; Lamar Wheat, Georgia Tech; Jack Little, Texas A&M

GUARDS-LINEBACKERS—Bob Ward, Maryland; Les Richter, California; Ray Beck, Georgia Tech; Marv Matuszak, Tulsa; Joe Palumbo, Virginia; George Mrkonic, Kansas; Ted Daffer, Tennessee; Nick Liotta, Villanova; Chet Millett, Holy Cross

CENTERS-LINEBACKERS—Dick Hightower, Southern Methodist; Doug Moseley, Kentucky; Keith Flowers, Texas Christian; Pat Cannamela, Southern California

BACKS—Dick Kazmaier, Princeton; Hank Lauricella, Tennessee; John Karras, Illinois; Vito Parilli, Kentucky; Larry Isbell, Baylor; Ollie Matson, San Francisco; Bobby Dillon, Texas; Al Brosky, Illinois; Hugh McElhenny, Washington; Frank Gifford, Southern California; Ed Modzelewski, Maryland; Gary Kerkorian, Stanford; Al Dorow, Michigan State

1952

ENDS—Frank McPhee, Princeton; Bernie Flowers, Purdue; Tom Stolhandske, Texas; Ed Bell, Pennsylvania; Don Branby, Colorado; Tom Scott, Virginia; Buck Martin, Georgia Tech; Joe Collier, Northwestern; Don Voss, Wisconsin

TACKLES—Dick Modzelewski, Maryland; Hal Miller, Georgia Tech; Doug Atkins, Tennessee; Kline Gilbert, Mississippi; David Suminski, Wisconsin; J.D. Kimmel, Houston; Charles LaPradd, Florida; Bob Fleck, Syracuse; Ed Meadows, Duke; Harvey Achziger, Colorado A&M; Jerry Minnick, Nebraska; Eldred Kraemer, Pittsburgh

GUARDS-LINEBACKERS—John Michels, Tennessee; Elmer Willhoite, Southern California; Harley Sewell, Texas; Frank Kush, Michigan State; Steve Eisenhauer, Navy; Marv Matuszak, Tulsa; Mike Takacs, Ohio State; Joe Schmidt, Pittsburgh

CENTERS-LINEBACKERS—Donn Moomaw, UCLA; Tom Catlin, Oklahoma; Dick Tamburo, Michigan State; Pete Brown, Georgia Tech; George Morris, Georgia Tech

BACKS—John Lattner, Notre Dame; Jack Scarbath, Maryland; Billy Vessels, Oklahoma; Jim Sears, Southern California; Leon Hardeman, Georgia Tech; Paul Giel, Minnesota; Bobby Moorhead, Georgia Tech; Don McAuliffe, Michigan State; Don Heinrich, Washington; John Olszewski, California; Buck McPhail, Oklahoma; Gene Filipski, Villanova; Gil Reich, Kansas

1953

ENDS—Don Dohoney, Michigan State; Carlton Massey, Texas; Steve Meilinger, Kentucky; Sam Morley, Stanford; Joe Collier, Northwestern; Ken Buck, College of the Pacific; John Carson, Georgia

TACKLES—Stan Jones, Maryland; Art Hunter, Notre Dame; Jack Shanafelt, Pennsylvania; Jim Smith, Baylor; Ed Meadows, Duke

GUARDS—J. D. Roberts, Oklahoma; Crawford Mims, Mississippi; Bob Fleck, Syracuse; Ray Correll, Kentucky; Milt Bohart, Washington; Steve Eisenhauer, Navy

CENTERS—Larry Morris, Georgia Tech; Matt Hazeltine, California; Jerry Hilgenberg, Iowa

BACKS—John Lattner, Notre Dame; Paul Giel, Minnesota; Paul Cameron, UCLA; J. C. Caroline, Illinois; Bob Garrett, Stanford; David Johnson, Rice; Bernie Faloney, Maryland; Alan Ameche, Wisconsin; Jackie Parker, Mississippi State

1954

ENDS—Max Boydston, Oklahoma; Ron Beagle, Navy; Don Holleder, Army; Frank McDonald, Miami, Fla.; Dean Dugger, Ohio State
TACKLES—Jack Ellena, UCLA; Sid Fournet, Louisiana State; Art Walker, Michigan; Darris McCord, Tennessee; Bud Brooks, Arkansas; Rex Boggan, Mississippi
GUARDS—Bud Brooks, Arkansas; Calvin Jones, Iowa; Tom Bettis, Purdue; Jim Salsbury, UCLA; Ralph Chesnauskas, Army; Frank Mincevich, South Carolina
CENTERS—Kurt Burris, Oklahoma; Matt Hazeltine, California
BACKS—Howard Cassady, Ohio State; Ralph Guglielmi, Notre Dame; Alan Ameche, Wisconsin; Dicky Moegle, Rice; Tommy Bell, Army; Bob Davenport, UCLA; Paul Larson, California; Bob McNamara, Minnesota

1955

ENDS—Ron Beagle, Navy; Ron Kramer, Michigan; Rommie Loudd, UCLA; Harold Burnine, Missouri; Howard Schnellenberger, Kentucky
TACKLES—Bruce Bosley, West Virginia; Norman Masters, Michigan State; Frank D'Agostino, Auburn; Hardiman Cureton, UCLA; Paul Wiggin, Stanford; John Witte, Oregon State; Sam Huff, West Virginia; Herb Gray, Texas
GUARDS—Bo Bolinger, Oklahoma; Calvin Jones, Iowa; Hardiman Cureton, UCLA; James Brown, UCLA; Pat Bisceglia, Notre Dame; Jim Parker, Ohio State; Tony Sardisco, Tulane
CENTERS—Bob Pellegrini, Maryland; Hugh Pitts, Texas Christian
BACKS—Howard Cassady, Ohio State; Jim Swink, Texas Christian; Paul Hornung, Notre Dame; Earl Morrall, Michigan State; Don Schaefer, Notre Dame; Jon Arnett, Southern California; Tommy McDonald, Oklahoma; Art Davis, Mississippi State; Joe Childress, Auburn; Bob Davenport, UCLA

1956

ENDS—Ron Kramer, Michigan; Joe Walton, Pittsburgh; Buddy Cruze, Tennessee; Bill Steiger, Washington State
TACKLES—John Witte, Oregon State; Lou Michaels, Kentucky; Alex Karras, Iowa; Charles Krueger, Texas A&M; Norman Hamilton, Texas Christian; Bob Hobert, Minnesota
GUARDS—Jim Parker, Ohio State; Bill Glass, Baylor; Sam Valentine, Penn State; John Barrow, Florida
CENTERS—Jerry Tubbs, Oklahoma; Don Stephenson, Georgia Tech
BACKS—Jimmy Brown, Syracuse; Johnny Majors, Tennessee; Tom McDonald, Oklahoma; John Brodie, Stanford; Paul Hornung, Notre Dame; Jim Crawford, Wyoming; Don Bosseler, Miami, Fla.; Bill Barnes, Wake Forest; Jack Pardee, Texas A&M

1957

ENDS—Jimmy Phillips, Auburn; Dick Wallen, UCLA; Jim Gibbons, Iowa; Fred Dugan, Dayton
TACKLES—Lou Michaels, Kentucky; Alex Karras, Iowa; Charles Krueger, Texas A&M; Tom Topping, Duke; Bob Reifsnyder, Navy
GUARDS—Bill Krisher, Oklahoma; Aurelius Thomas, Ohio State; Al Ecuyer, Notre Dame; Jack Simpson, Mississippi; Bill Johnson, Tennessee
CENTERS—Dan Currie, Michigan State; Don Stephenson, Georgia Tech; Bob Reifsnyder, Navy
BACKS—John Crow, Texas A&M; Bob Anderson, Army; Walt Kowalczyk, Michigan State; King Hill, Rice; Clendon Thomas, Oklahoma; Bob Stransky, Colorado; Jim Pace, Michigan; Dick Christy, North Carolina State; Tom Forrestal, Navy; Lee Grosscup, Utah; Jim Bakhtiar, Virginia; Jimmy Taylor, Louisiana State

1958

ENDS—Buddy Dial, Rice; Sam Williams, Michigan State; Jim Houston, Ohio State; Al Goldstein, North Carolina; Curt Merz, Iowa; Jim Wood, Oklahoma State
TACKLES—Ted Bates, Oregon State; Brock Strom, Air Force; Andy Cvercko, Northwestern; Don Floyd, Texas Christian; Vel Heckman, Florida; Gene Selawski, Purdue; Hogan Wharton, Houston
GUARDS—George Deiderich, Vanderbilt; John Guzik, Pittsburgh; Zeke Smith, Auburn; Al Ecuyer, Notre Dame; Bob Novogratz, Army; John Wooten, Colorado
CENTERS—Bob Harrison, Oklahoma; Max Fugler, Louisiana State; Jackie Burkett, Auburn
BACKS—Randy Duncan, Iowa; Pete Dawkins, Army; Billy Cannon, Louisiana State; Billy White, Ohio State; Nick Pietrosante, Notre Dame; Billy Austin, Rutgers; Bob Anderson, Army; Joe Kapp, California; Don Meredith, Southern Methodist

1959

ENDS—Bill Carpenter, Army; Marlin McKeever, Southern California; Fred Mautino, Syracuse; Monty Stickles, Notre Dame; Don Norton, Iowa; Carroll Dale, Virginia Tech; Chris Burford, Stanford
TACKLERS—Dan Lanphear, Wisconsin; Don Floyd, Texas Christian; Mike McGee, Duke; Ken Rice, Auburn
GUARDS—Roger Davis, Syracuse; Bill Burrell, Illinois; Maurice Doke, Texas; Pat Dye, Georgia; Marvin Terrell, Mississippi; Zeke Smith, Auburn
CENTERS—Maxie Baughan, Georgia Tech; Jim Andreotti, Northwestern; Emil J. Holub, Texas Tech
BACKS—Billy Cannon, Louisiana State; Charley Flowers, Mississippi; Richie Lucas, Penn State; Ron Burton, Northwestern; Bob Schloredt, Washington; Jim Mooty, Arkansas; Dean Look, Michigan State; Don Meredith, Southern Methodist; Dwight Nichols, Iowa State; Jack Spikes, Texas Christian

1960

ENDS—Mike Ditka, Pittsburgh; Danny LaRose, Missouri; Claude (Tee) Moorman, Duke; Bill Miller, Miami, Fla.
TACKLES—Bob Lilly, Texas Christian; Ken Rice, Auburn; Merlin Olsen, Utah State; Jerry Beabout, Purdue
GUARDS—Tom Brown, Minnesota; Joe Romig, Colorado; Ben Balme, Yale; Mark Manders, Iowa; Wayne Harris, Arkansas
CENTERS—Emil J. Holub, Texas Tech; Roy McKasson, Washington
BACKS—Joe Bellino, Navy; Bob Ferguson, Ohio State; Jake Gibbs, Mississippi; Ernie Davis, Syracuse; Pervis Atkins, New Mexico State; Bill Kilmer, UCLA; Ed Dyas, Auburn; Roman Gabriel, North Carolina State; John Hadl, Kansas; Larry Ferguson, Iowa

1961

ENDS—Gary Collins, Maryland; Bill Miller, Miami, Fla.; Jerry Hillebrand, Colorado; Bob Mitinger, Penn State; Greg Mather, Navy; Pat Richter, Wisconsin
TACKLES—Billy Neighbors, Alabama; Merlin Olsen, Utah State; Bobby Bell, Minnesota; Don Talbert, Texas; Ed Blaine, Missouri
GUARDS—Roy Winston, Louisiana State; Joe Romig, Colorado; Dave Behrman, Michigan State
CENTERS—Alex Kroll, Rutgers; Ron Hull, UCLA
BACKS—Ernie Davis, Syracuse; Jimmy Saxton, Texas; Bob Ferguson, Ohio State; Sandy Stephens, Minnesota; Roman Gabriel, North Carolina State; John Hadl, Kansas; Lance Alworth, Arkansas; Billy Ray Adams, Mississippi

1962

ENDS—Pat Richter, Wisconsin; Hal Bedsole, Southern California; Dave Robinson, Penn State; Conrad Hitchler, Missouri
TACKLES—Bobby Bell, Minnesota; Don Brumm, Purdue; Steve Barnett, Oregon; Fred Miller, Louisiana State; Jim Dunaway, Mississippi
GUARDS—Johnny Treadwell, Texas; Rufus Guthrie, Georgia Tech; Damon Bame, Southern California; Jean Berry, Duke; Leon Cross, Oklahoma; Jack Cvercko, Northwestern
CENTERS—Lee Roy Jordan, Alabama; Don McKinnon, Dartmouth
BACKS—Terry Baker, Oregon State; Jerry Stovall, Louisiana State; George Saimes, Michigan State; George Mira, Miami, Fla.; Mel Renfro, Oregon; Roger Kochman, Penn State; Bill Moore, Arkansas; Tom Myers, Northwestern; Glynn Griffing, Mississippi; Dave Hoppmann, Iowa State

1963

ENDS—Vern Burke, Oregon State; Lawrence Elkins, Baylor; Jim Kelly, Notre Dame; Bob Lacey, No. Carolina; Bill Martin, Ga. Tech; Dave Parks, Texas Tech
TACKLES—Scott Appleton, Texas; Carl Eller, Minnesota; Ernie Borghetti, Pitt; Ken Kortas, Louisville; Harry Schuh, Memphis State

GUARDS—Bob Brown, Nebraska; Rick Redman, Washington; Damon Bame, So. Calif.; Steve DeLong, Tenn.; Mike Reilly, Iowa; Herschel Turner, Kentucky
CENTERS—Dick Butkus, Ill.; Ken Dill, Miss.
BACKS—Roger Staubach, Navy; Sherman Lewis, Mich. State; Jim Grisham, Oklahoma; Gale Sayers, Kansas; Paul Martha, Pittsburgh; Tom Crutcher, TCU; Tom Ford, Texas; Billy Lothridge, Ga. Tech; Mel Renfro, Oregon; Jim Sidle, Auburn; Don Trull, Baylor; Tom Vaughn, Iowa State; Jay Wilkinson, Duke

1964

ENDS—Jack Snow, Notre Dame; Fred Biletnikoff, Florida State; Harold Wells, Purdue; Allen Brown, Mississippi; Alphonse Dotson, Grambling; Al Atkinson, Villanova; Ray Rissmiller, Georgia
TACKLES—Larry Kramer, Nebraska; Ralph Neely, Oklahoma; Steve DeLong, Tennessee; Jim Wilson, Georgia; Bill Yearby, Michigan; Dan Kearly, Alabama; John Van Sicklen, Iowa State; Remi Prudhomme, Louisiana State; Stas Maliszewski, Princeton; Jim Davidson, Ohio State; Harry Schuh, Memphis State
GUARDS—Rick Redman, Washington; Glenn Ressler, Penn State; Tommy Nobis, Texas; Ronnie Caveness, Arkansas; Bill Fisk, Southern Calif.; Wayne Freeman, Alabama; Carl McAdams, Oklahoma; Jack O'Billovich, Oregon State; Don Croftcheck, Indiana; Jim Carroll, Notre Dame
CENTERS—Dick Butkus, Ill.; Dwight Kelley, Ohio State; Pat Killorin, Syracuse; Malcolm Walker, Rice
BACKS—John Huarte, Notre Dame; Gale Sayers, Kansas; Larry Elkins, Baylor; Tucker Frederickson, Auburn; Jerry Rhome, Tulsa; Jim Grabowski, Ill.; Craig Morton, California; Clarence Williams, Washington State; Donny Anderson, Texas Tech; Cosmo Iacavazzi, Princeton; Bob Berry, Oregon; Larry Dupree, Florida; Tom Nowatzke, Indiana; Floyd Little, Syracuse; Bob Schweickert, VPI; Bob Timberlake, Michigan; Arnold Chonko, Ohio State; Karl Noonan, Iowa; Mike Garrett, Southern Calif.; Roy Jefferson, Utah; George Donnelly, Illinois; Gerry Bussell, Georgia Tech

1965

ENDS—Howard Twilley, Tulsa; Aaron Brown, Minnesota; Freeman White, Nebraska; Charles Smith, Mich. State; Chuck Casey, Florida; Gene Washington, Mich. State; Bobby Crockett, Arkansas; Tony Jeter, Nebraska; Ed Weisacosky, Miami (Fla.); Lynn Matthews, Florida
TACKLES—Sam Ball, Kentucky; Walt Barnes, Nebraska; Glen Ray Hines, Arkansas; Loyd Phillips, Arkansas; Karl Singer, Purdue; Jack Thornton, Auburn; Wayne Foster, Washington State; George Patton, Georgia; Harold Lucas, Mich. State
GUARDS—Dick Arrington, Notre Dame; Bill Yearby, Michigan; Stas Maliszewski, Princeton; Carl McAdams, Oklahoma; Ron Goovert, Mich. State; Doug Van Horn, Ohio State; Jerry Shay, Purdue

116

CENTERS—Paul Crane, Alabama; Tommy Nobis, Texas; Dwight Kelley, Ohio State
BACKS—Bob Griese, Purdue; Frank Emanuel, Tennessee; Donny Anderson, Texas Tech; George Webster, Mich. State; Mike Garrett, Southern Calif.; Johnny Roland, Missouri; Jim Grabowski, Illinois; Nick Rassas, Notre Dame; Floyd Little, Syracuse; Steve Juday, Mich. State; Clinton Jones, Mich. State; Steve Spurrier, Florida; Bruce Bennett, Florida

1966

ENDS—Jack Clancy, Michigan; Alan Page, Notre Dame; Ray Perkins, Alabama; Charles Smith, Mich. State; Gene Washington, Mich. State; Austin Denney, Tennessee; Jim Bierne, Purdue
TACKLES—Cecil Dowdy, Alabama; Loyd Phillips, Arkansas; Ron Yary, Southern Calif.; Tom Greenlee, Washington; Maurice Moorman, Texas A&M; Wayne Mass, Clemson; Jerry West, Mich. State; Dennis Byrd, N.C. State; Pete Duranko, Notre Dame; George Patton, Georgia
GUARDS—Tom Regner, Notre Dame; Wayne Meylan, Nebraska; LaVerne Allers, Nebraska; John LaGrone, SMU; Gary Bugenhagen, Syracuse; Ed Chandler, Georgia; John Richardson, UCLA
CENTERS—Jim Breland, Georgia Tech; Paul Naumoff, Tennessee; Ray Pryor, Ohio State; Townsend Clarke, Army; Bob Matheson, Duke
BACKS—Steve Spurrier, Florida; Jim Lynch, Notre Dame; Nick Eddy, Notre Dame; George Webster, Mich. State; Mel Farr, UCLA; Tom Beier, Miami (Fla.); Clint Jones, Mich. State; Nate Shaw, So. Calif.; Lenny Snow, Georgia Tech; Bob Griese, Purdue; Floyd Little, Syracuse; Larry Csonka, Syracuse; Frank Loria, Virginia Tech; Larry Wachholtz, Nebraska; Martine Bercher, Arkansas; Bobby Johns, Alabama; Wynn Mabry, Dartmouth

1967

ENDS—Dennis Homan, Alabama; Ted Hendricks, Miami, (Fla.) Ron Sellers, Florida State; Tim Rossovich, So. Calif.; Ken Hebert, Houston; Ted Kwalick, Penn State; Jim Seymour, Notre Dame; Bob Stein, Minnesota; John Garlington, LSU

TACKLES—Ed Chandler, Georgia; Dennis Byrd, N.C. State; Ron Yary, So. Calif.; Granville Liggins, Oklahoma; Larry Slagle, UCLA; Mike Dirks, Wyoming; Jon Sandstrom, Oregon State; Kevin Hardy, Notre Dame; Jess Lewis, Oregon State; Bill Staley, Utah State
GUARDS—Harry Olszewski, Clemson; Wayne Meylan, Nebraska; Rich Stotter, Houston; Adrian Young, So. Calif.; Gary Cassells, Indiana; Phil Tucker, Texas Tech; Bob Kalsu, Oklahoma; Greg Pipes, Baylor
CENTERS—Bob Johnson, Tennessee; Don Manning, UCLA
BACKS—Gary Beban, UCLA; Frank Loria, Va. Tech; Leroy Keyes, Purdue; Tom Schoen, Notre Dame; O. J. Simpson, So. Calif.; Bobby Johns, Alabama; Larry Csonka, Syracuse; Dick Anderson, Colorado; Corby Robertson, Texas; D. D. Lewis, Miss. State; Fred Carr, UTex (El Paso); Tom Beutler, Toledo; Bill Hobbs, Texas A&M; Fred Combs, N.C. State; Al Dorsey, Tennessee; Jim Smith, Oregon; Harry Cheatwood, Okla. State

1968

ENDS—Ron Sellers, Florida State; Jim Seymour, Notre Dame; Jerry Levias, Southern Methodist; Ted Hendricks, Miami, Fla.; John Zook, Kansas; Ted Kwalick, Penn State
TACKLES—Dave Foley, Ohio State; George Kunz, Notre Dame; Bill Stanfill, Georgia; Joe Green, N. Texas State; Rufus Mayes, Ohio State; Rolf Krueger, Texas A&M
GUARDS—Charles Rosenfelder, Tennessee; John Shinners, Xavier; Mike Montler, Colorado; Jim Barnes, Arkansas; Joe Armstrong, Nebraska; Guy Dennis, Florida; Mal Snider, Stanford; Bob Babich, Miami of Ohio; Ron Pritchard, Arizona State; Ed White, California; Chuck Kyle, Purdue; Dennis Onkotz, Penn State; Steve Kiner, Tennessee; Mike Widger, Virginia Tech
CENTER—John Didion, Oregon State
BACKS—O. J. Simpson, Southern California; Terry Hanratty, Notre Dame; Bob Douglass, Kansas; Leroy Keyes, Purdue; Paul Gipson, Houston; Chris Gilbert, Texas; Ron Johnson, Michigan; Bill Enyart, Oregon State; Jake Scott, Georgia; Roger Wehrli, Missouri; Jim Marsalis, Tennessee A&I; Al Worley, Washington; Larry Smith, Florida; Tom Maxwell, Texas A&M

COLLEGE PLAYERS ELECTED TO THE
NATIONAL FOOTBALL FOUNDATION
HALL OF FAME

*(Players become eligible for consideration by the Founda-
tion's Honors Court after 10 years following graduation.)*

NAME	COLLEGE	POSITION	YEARS PLAYED	DATE OF ELECTION
Alex Agase	Purdue	Guard	1943	
	U. of Illinois	Guard	1942-1946	1963
Frank Albert	Stanford	Quarterback	1939-1941	1956
Charles (Ki) Aldrich	Texas Christian	Center	1936-1938	1960
Joseph Alexander	Syracuse	Guard	1918-1920	1954
Clarence Everett Bacon	Wesleyan University	Quarterback	1909-1912	1966
Stanley N. Barnes	California	End	1918-1921	1954
Charles Barrett	Cornell	Quarterback	1913-1915	1958
Bert Baston	Minnesota	End	1914-1916	1954
Clifford F. Battles	W. Va. Wesleyan	Halfback	1929-1931	1955
Samuel Baugh	Texas Christian	Halfback	1934-1936	1951
James Bausch	Kansas	Halfback	1929-1930	1954
John J. Berwanger	Chicago	Quarterback	1933-1935	1954
Felix (Doc) Blanchard	Army	Fullback	1944-1946	1959
Lynn Bomar	Vanderbilt	End	1921-1924	1956
Albert (Albie) Booth	Yale	Halfback	1929-1931	1966
Fred (Buzz) Borries, Jr.	Navy	Halfback	1932-1934	1960
Benny Lee Boynton	Williams	Quarterback	1917-19, 1920	1962
Gordon F. Brown	Yale	Guard	1897-1900	1954
John H. (Babe) Brown, Jr.	Navy	Guard	1910-1913	1951
John Mack Brown	Alabama	Halfback	1923-1925	1957

NAME	COLLEGE	POSITION	YEARS PLAYED	DATE OF ELECTION
Christian K. Cagle	Army	Halfback	1926-1929	1954
David C. Campbell	Harvard	End	1899-1901	1958
John (Jack) Cannon	Notre Dame	Guard	1927-1929	1965
Frank Carideo	Notre Dame	Quarterback	1928-1930	1954
Charles (Chuck) R. Carney	Univ. of Illinois	End	1918-1921	1966
C. Hunter Carpenter	V.P.I.	Halfback	1900-03, 1905	1957
Charles (Chuck) Carroll	Washington	Halfback	1926-1928	1964
Edward L. Casey	Harvard	Halfback	1916-1919	1968
Guy Chamberlin	Nebraska	Halfback	1913-1915	1962
Paul Christman	Missouri	Halfback	1938-1940	1956
Earl (Dutch) Clark	Colorado College	Quarterback	1927-1929	1951
Charles (Chuck) A. Conerly	Univ. of Mississippi	Tailback	1942, 47, 48	1966
George Connor	Holy Cross	Tackle	1942-1943	
	Notre Dame	Tackle	1946-1947	1963
William Corbus	Stanford	Guard	1931-1933	1957
Hector W. Cowan	Princeton	Tackle	1885-1889	1951
Edward H. (Ted) Coy	Yale	Fullback	1907-1909	1951
James (Jim) Crowley	Notre Dame	Halfback	1922-1924	1966
Slade D. Cutter	U.S. Naval Acad.	Tackle	1932-1934	1967
Gerald Dalrymple	Tulane	End	1929-1931	1954
Charles D. Daly	Harvard	Quarterback	1898-1900	
	Army	Quarterback	1901-1902	1951
Glenn Davis	Army	Halfback	1943-1946	1961
Paul R. DesJardien	Chicago	Center	1912-1914	1955
John R. DeWitt	Princeton	Guard	1901-1903	1954
Robert Lee (Bobby) Dodd	Tennessee	Quarterback	1928-1930	1959
Nathan W. Dougherty	Univ. of Tennessee	Guard	1907-1909	1967
Morley Drury	Southern California	Quarterback	1925-1927	1954
William M. Dudley	Virginia	Halfback	1939-1941	1956
Walter H. Eckersall	Chicago	Quarterback	1904-1906	1951
Ray Evans	Kansas	Halfback	1941-1942	
			1946-1947	1964
William Beattie Feathers	Tennessee	Halfback	1931-1933	1955
Wesley E. Fesler	Ohio State	End	1928-1930	1954
Hamilton Fish	Harvard	Tackle	1907-1909	1954
A. R. (Buck) Flowers	Georgia Tech	Halfback	1918-1920	1955
Clinton E. Frank	Yale	Halfback	1935-1937	1955
Benjamin Friedman	Michigan	Quarterback	1924-1926	1951
Edgar W. Garbisch	Wash. & Jefferson	Guard	1917-1920	
	Army	Center	1921-1924	1954
Charles Gelbert	Pennsylvania	End	1894-1896	1960
Walter Gilbert	Auburn	Center	1934-1936	1956

NAME	COLLEGE	POSITION	YEARS PLAYED	DATE OF ELECTION
George Gipp	Notre Dame	Fullback	1917-1920	1951
Marshall Goldberg	Pittsburgh	Halfback	1936-1938	1958
Otto Graham	Northwestern	Halfback	1941-1943	1956
Harold E. (Red) Grange	Illinois	Halfback	1923-1925	1951
Robert H. Grayson	Stanford	Fullback	1933-1935	1955
Merle A. Gulick	Toledo	Quarterback	1925	
	Hobart	Quarterback	1927-1929	1965
Edwin (Goat) Hale	Mississippi College	Halfback	1915-1916	
			1920-1921	1963
Thomas J. Hamilton	U. S. Naval Acad.	Halfback	1924-1926	1965
H. R. (Tack) Hardwick	Harvard	End	1912-1914	1954
T. Truxton Hare	Pennsylvania	Guard	1897-1900	1951
Charles W. (Chic) Harley	Ohio State	Halfback	1916-1919	1951
Thomas D. Harmon	Michigan	Halfback	1938-1940	1954
Howard Harpster	Carnegie Tech	Quarterback	1926-1928	1956
Edward J. Hart	Princeton	Tackle	1909-1911	1954
Homer H. Hazel	Rutgers	Fullback	1922-1924	1951
W. W. (Pudge) Heffelfinger	Yale	Guard	1888-1891	1951
Melvin J. Hein	Washington State	Center	1928-1930	1954
Wilbur F. (Fats) Henry	Wash. & Jefferson	Tackle	1917-1919	1951
Robert John Herwig	California	Center	1935-1937	1964
William M. Heston	Michigan	Halfback	1901-1904	1954
Heman Michael Hickman	Tennessee	Guard	1929-1931	1959
Dan (Tiger) Hill	Duke	Center	1936-1938	1962
Frank A. Hinkey	Yale	End	1891-1894	1951
Carl Hinkle	Vanderbilt	Center	1935-1937	1959
James Hitchcock	Auburn	Halfback	1930-1932	1954
James J. Hogan	Yale	Tackle	1902-1904	1954
Jerome H. (Brud) Holland	Cornell	End	1936-1938	1965
William M. Hollenback	Pennsylvania	Halfback	1906-1908	1951
Robert C. (Cal) Hubbard	Centenary	Tackle	1922-1924	
	Geneva	End	1926	1962
John Houghton Hubbard	Amherst	Halfback	1903-1906	1966
Allison (Pooley) Hubert	Alabama	Fullback	1922-1925	1964
Weldon G. Humble	Rice	Guard	1941-42, 1946	1961
Joel Hunt	Texas A & M	Halfback	1925	
		Quarterback	1926-1927	1967
Donald Hutson	Alabama	End	1932-1934	1951
Cecil F. Isbell	Purdue	Back	1935-1937	1967
Herbert Joesting	Minnesota	Fullback	1925-1927	1954
Frank Alexander Juhan	Univ. of the South	Center	1908-1910	1966
Charles (Choo Choo) Justice	North Carolina	Halfback	1946-1949	1961

NAME	COLLEGE	POSITION	YEARS PLAYED	DATE OF ELECTION
Ken Kavanaugh	Louisiana State U.	End	1937-1939	1963
Edgar L. Kaw	Cornell	Halfback	1920-1922	1954
Richard William Kazmaier	Princeton	Halfback	1949-1951	1966
James Stanton Keck	Princeton	Tackle	1920-1921	1959
Henry H. Ketcham	Yale	Center	1911-1913	1968
John Reed Kilpatrick	Yale	End	1908-1910	1955
John C. Kimbrough	Texas A & M	Fullback	1938-1940	1954
Frank (Bruiser) Kinard	Mississippi	Tackle	1935-1937	1951
Philip King	Princeton	Quarterback	1890-1893	1962
Nile Kinnick	Iowa	Halfback	1937-1939	1951
Harry Kipke	Michigan	Halfback	1921-1923	1958
Elmer F. Layden	Notre Dame	Halfback	1922-1924	1951
Bobby Layne	Texas	Quarterback	1945-1947	1968
Langdon (Biffy) Lea	Princeton	Tackle & End	1892-1895	1964
James Leech	V.M.I.	Halfback	1919-1920	1956
Gordon C. Locke	Iowa	Fullback	1920-1922	1960
Sid Luckman	Columbia	Quarterback	1936-1938	1960
John Lujack	Notre Dame	Quarterback	1943, 46-47.	1960
Francis L. (Pug) Lund	Minnesota	Halfback	1932-1934	1958
Edward W. Mahan	Harvard	Fullback	1913-1915	1951
William N. (Memphis Bill) Mallory	Yale	Fullback	1921-1923	1964
J. L. (Pete) Mauthe	Penn State	Halfback	1910-1912	1957
George A. McAfee	Duke	Halfback	1937-1939	1961
Thomas Lee (Bum) McClung	Yale	Halfback	1889-1891	1963
James B. McCormick	Princeton	Fullback	1905-1907	1954
Eugene T. McEver	Tennessee	Halfback	1928, 29, 31	1954
John J. McEwan	Army	Center	1914-1916	1962
James Banks McFadden	Clemson	Halfback	1937-1939	1959
John Francis McGovern	Univ. of Minnesota	Quarterback	1908-1910	1966
George W. (Tank) McLaren	Univ. of Pittsburgh	Fullback	1915-1918	1965
Alvin (Bo) McMillin	Centre	Quarterback	1919-1921	1951
Robert McWhorter	Georgia	Halfback	1910-1913	1954
E. LeRoy Mercer	Pennsylvania	Fullback	1910-1912	1955
Abe Mickal	Louisiana State U.	Halfback	1933-1935	1967
Edgar E. (Rip) Miller	Notre Dame	Tackle	1922-1924	1966
John H. Minds	Pennsylvania	Fullback	1894-1897	1962
Cliff Montgomery	Columbia	Quarterback	1931-1933	1963
Harold (Brick) Muller	California	End	1920-1922	1951
Bronko Nagurski	Minnesota	Tackle	1927-1929	1951
Ernest A. Nevers	Stanford	Fullback	1923-1925	1951
Marshall Newell	Harvard	Tackle	1890-1893	1957

NAME	COLLEGE	POSITION	YEARS PLAYED	DATE OF ELECTION
Andrew J. Oberlander	Dartmouth	Halfback	1923-1925	1954
Robert David O'Brien	Texas Christian	Halfback	1936-1938	1955
Pat O'Dea	Wisconsin	Fullback	1897-1899	1962
Elmer Oliphant	Purdue	Halfback	1911-1913	
	Army	Halfback	1915-1917	1955
Benjamin G. Oosterbaan	Michigan	End	1925-1927	1954
Clarence (Ace) Parker	Duke	Halfback	1934-1936	1955
Vincent (Pat) Pazzetti	Wesleyan	Quarterback	1908-1909	
	Lehigh	Quarterback	1910-1912	1961
Robert Peck	Pittsburgh	Center	1914-1916	1954
Stanley B. Pennock	Harvard	Guard	1912-1914	1954
George R. Pfann	Cornell	Quarterback	1921-1923	1957
Henry Disbrow Phillips	U. of the South	Guard	1901-1904	1959
Peter L. (Pete) Pihos	Indiana Univ.	End-Fullback	1942, 43, 45, 46	1966
Ernie Pinckert	Southern California	Halfback	1929-1931	1957
John Pingel	Michigan State	Halfback	1936-1938	1968
Frederick (Fritz) Pollard	Brown	Halfback	1914-1916	1954
Henry R. (Peter) Pund	Georgia Tech	Center	1926-1928	1963
Claude Reeds	Oklahoma	Fullback	1910-1913	1961
Robert (Horse) Reynolds	Stanford	Tackle	1933-1935	1961
Charles (Babe) Rinehart	Lafayette	Guard	1894-1897	1964
Aaron David Rosenberg	Southern California	Guard	1931-1933	1966
Ira E. Rodgers	West Virginia	Fullback	1917-1919	1957
(William) Kyle Rote	S.M.U.	Halfback	1948-1950	1964
Joseph Routt	Texas A & M	Guard	1935-1937	1962
George H. Sauer	Nebraska	Fullback	1931-1933	1954
Wear K. Schoonover	Univ. of Arkansas	End	1927-1929	1967
David N. Schreiner	Wisconsin	End	1940-1942	1955
Adolf (Germany) Schulz	Michigan	Center	1905-1908	1951
Frank J. Schwab	Lafayette	Guard	1919-1922	1958
Paul Schwegler	U. of Washington	Tackle	1929-1931	1967
Thomas L. Shevlin	Yale	End	1903-1905	1954
Claude (Monk) Simons	Tulane	Halfback	1932-1934	1968
Frederick W. Sington	Alabama	Tackle	1928-1930	1955
Frank Sinkwich	Georgia	Halfback	1940-1942	1954
F. F. (Duke) Slater	Iowa	Tackle	1918-1921	1951
Harry Smith	Southern California	Guard	1937-1939	1955
Neil Snow	Michigan	Halfback	1898-1901	1960
Clarence W. Spears	Dartmouth	Guard	1914-1915	1955
W. D. (Bill) Spears	Vanderbilt	Quarterback	1925-1927	1962
William Earl Sprackling	Brown	Quarterback	1908-1911	1964
Amos Alonzo Stagg	Yale	End	1885-1889	1951

NAME	COLLEGE	POSITION	YEARS PLAYED	DATE OF ELECTION
Herb Stein	Pittsburgh	Center	1918-1921	1967
Kenneth Strong	N. Y. U.	Fullback	1926-1928	1957
Harry Stuhldreher	Notre Dame	Quarterback	1922-1924	1958
Robert L. Suffridge	Tennessee	Guard	1938-1940	1961
James Thorpe	Carlisle	Halfback	1908, 11, 12	1951
Benjamin H. Ticknor	Harvard	Center	1928-1930	1954
Gaynell Tinsley	Louisiana State	End	1934-1936	1956
Eric (The Red) Tipton	Duke	Back	1936-1938	1965
Charles Trippi	Georgia	Halfback	1945-1946	1959
J. Edward (Eddie) Tryon	Colgate	Halfback	1922-1925	1963
Clyde (Bulldog) Turner	Hardin-Simmons	Center	1937-1939	1960
Norman VanBrocklin	Oregon	Quarterback	1947-1948	1966
Ewell Doak Walker	S. M. U.	Quarterback	1946-1949	1959
Adam Walsh	Notre Dame	Center	1922-1924	1968
Kenneth Washington	U.C.L.A.	Halfback	1937-1939	1956
Harold H. Weekes	Columbia	Halfback	1900-1902	1954
Ed Weir	Nebraska	Tackle	1923-1925	1951
John A. C. Weller	Princeton	Guard	1933-1935	1957
D. Belford West	Colgate	Tackle	1915, 16, 19	1954
Charles (Buck) Wharton	Pennsylvania	Guard	1893-1896	1963
Byron (Whizzer) White	Colorado	Halfback	1936-1938	1954
Donald Whitmire	Alabama	Tackle	1941-1942	
	Navy	Tackle	1943-1944	1956
Edwin Widseth	Minnesota	Tackle	1934-1936	1954
Richard Wildung	Minnesota	Tackle	1940-1942	1957
James A. (Froggy) Williams	Rice	End	1947-1949	1965
George Wilson	Washington	Halfback	1923-1925	1951
Albert A. Wistert	Michigan	Tackle	1940-1942	1968
Francis M. (Whitey) Wistert	Univ. of Michigan	Tackle	1931-1933	1967
Alexander Wojciechowicz	Fordham	Center	1934-1936	1955
Andrew R. E. Wyant	Bucknell	Center	1888-1891	
	Chicago	Guard	1892-1894	1962
Claude (Buddy) Young	Illinois	Halfback	1943-44, 46	1968
H. K. (Cy) Young	Washington & Lee	Halfback	1913-1916	1958

COLLEGE COACHES ELECTED TO THE
NATIONAL FOOTBALL FOUNDATION
HALL OF FAME

*(Coaches become eligible for consideration by the
Foundation's Honors Court three years after retirement.)*

NAME	COACHED AT	YEARS	YEAR ELECTED TO HALL OF FAME
William A. Alexander	Georgia Tech.	1921-1944	1951
Ike Armstrong	Utah	1925-1949	1957
Madison (Matty) Bell	Haskell Institute	1920-1921	
	Carroll College	1922	
	Texas Christian	1923-1928	
	Texas A & M	1929-1933	
	Southern Methodist	1935-1941	
		1945-1949	1955
Hugo Bezdek	Arkansas	1908-1912	
	Oregon	1913-1917	
	Penn State	1918-1929	1954
Dana X. Bible	Louisiana State U.	1916	
	Texas A & M	1917, 1919, 1928	
	Nebraska	1929-1936	
	Texas	1937-1945	1951
Bernard W. Bierman	Mississippi A & M	1925-1926	
	Tulane	1927-1932	
	Minnesota	1932-1941	
		1945-1950	1955
Earl (Red) Henry Blaik	Wisconsin	1926	
	Army	1927-1933	
	Dartmouth	1934-1940	
	Army	1941-1958	1964

NAME	COACHED AT	YEARS	YEAR ELECTED TO HALL OF FAME
Charles W. Caldwell, Jr.	Williams	1928-1942	
	Princeton	1945-1956	1961
Walter Camp	Yale	1888-1892	
	Stanford	1893, 1895	
	Yale (Advisory)	1882-1910	1951
Frank W. Cavanaugh	Holy Cross	1903-1905	
	Dartmouth	1911-1916	
	Boston College	1919-1926	
	Fordham	1927-1932	1954
Zora Clevenger	Indiana	1900-1903	1968
Herbert O. (Fritz) Crisler	Minnesota	1930-1931	
	Princeton	1932-1937	
	Michigan	1938-1947	1954
Gilmore Dobie	Washington	1908-1916	
	Navy	1917-1919	
	Cornell	1920-1935	
	Boston College	1936-1938	1951
Michael J. Donohue	Auburn	1904-1922	
	Louisiana State	1923-1927	1951
Charles E. (Gus) Dorais	Detroit	1925-1944	1954
Donald B. Faurot	Missouri	1925, 1935-1956	
	Kirksville	1926-1934	1961
Edward K. Hall	Illinois	1892-1893	1951
Richard C. Harlow	Penn State	1914-1917	
	Colgate	1922-1925	
	Western Maryland	1926-1934	
	Harvard	1935-1942	
		1945-1947	1954
Percy P. Haughton	Cornell	1899-1900	
	Harvard	1908-1916	
	Columbia	1923-1924	1951
John W. Heisman	Oberlin	1892-1894	
	Akron	1893	
	Auburn	1895-1899	
	Clemson	1900-1903	
	Georgia Tech	1904-1919	
	Pennsylvania	1920-1922	
	Wash. & Jefferson	1923	
	Rice	1924-1927	1954

NAME	COACHED AT	YEARS	YEAR ELECTED TO HALL OF FAME
Robert A. Higgins	W. Va. Wesleyan	1920-1924	
	Wash. (St. Louis)	1925-1927	
	Penn State	1930-1948	1954
Adm. Jonas H. Ingram	Navy	1904-06	1968
Howard H. Jones	Syracuse	1908	
	Yale	1909, 1913	
	Ohio State	1910	
	Iowa	1916-1923	
	Duke	1924	
	Southern California	1925-1940	1951
L. McC. (Biff) Jones	Army	1926-1929	
	Louisiana State	1932-1934	
	Oklahoma	1935-1936	
	Nebraska	1937-1942	1954
Thomas A. D. (Tad) Jones	Syracuse	1909-1910	
	Yale	1916, 1920-1927	1958
Andrew Kerr	Stanford	1922-1923	
	Wash. & Jefferson	1926-1928	
	Colgate	1929-1946	1951
George E. Little	Miami (Ohio)	1916-17, 1919-22	
	Wisconsin	1925-1927	
	Cincinnati	1914-1916	1955
Lou Little	Georgetown	1924-1929	
	Columbia	1930-1956	1960
Daniel McGugin	Vanderbilt	1904-1934	1951
DeOrmond (Tuss) McLaughry	Westminster	1915-1916, 1921	
	Amherst	1922-1925	
	Brown	1926-1940	
	Dartmouth	1941-1942	
		1945-1954	1962
L. R. (Dutch) Meyer	Texas Christian	1934-1952	1956
Bernie H. Moore	Louisiana State	1935-1947	1954
Ray Morrison	Southern Methodist	1915-16, 1922-34	
	Vanderbilt	1935-1939	
	Temple	1940-1948	
	Austin	1949-1952	1954
Clarence (Biggie) Munn	Albright	1935-1936	
	Syracuse	1946	
	Michigan State	1947-1953	1959

NAME	COACHED AT	YEARS	YEAR ELECTED TO HALL OF FAME
Earle (Greasy) Neale	Muskingum	1915	
	W. Va. Wesleyan	1916-1917	
	Marietta	1919-1920	
	Washington & Jefferson	1921-1922	
	Univ. of Virginia	1923-1928	
	West Virginia Univ.	1931-1933	
	Yale (Backfield Coach)	1934-1940	1967
Robert R. Neyland	Tennessee	1926-1934	
		1936-1940	
		1946-1952	1956
Frank J. (Buck) O'Neill	Colgate	1902	
	Syracuse	1906-1907	
	Columbia	1920-1922	1951
Bennie Owen	Oklahoma	1905-1926	1951
E. N. Robinson	Nebraska	1896-1897	
	Brown	1898-1901	
		1904-1907	
		1910-1925	1955
Knute K. Rockne	Notre Dame	1918-1931	1951
Edward L. Rogers	Carlisle	1896-1900	1968
	Minnesota	1901-1903	
E. L. (Dick) Romney	Utah State	1919-1948	1954
William W. Roper	Princeton	1906-1908	
	Missouri	1909	
	Princeton	1910-1911	
		1919-1930	1951
Clark D. Shaughnessy	Tulane	1922-1926	
	Chicago	1933-1939	
	Stanford	1940-1941	1968
Andrew L. Smith	Pennsylvania	1909-1912	
	Purdue	1913-1915	
	California	1916-1925	1951
Carl G. Snavely	Cincinnati	1919-1920	
	Marietta	1921	
	Bucknell	1927-1933	
	North Carolina	1934-35, 1945-52	
	Cornell	1936-1944	
	Washington (St. Louis)	1953-1958	1965
Amos Alonzo Stagg	Springfield	1890-1891	
	Chicago	1892-1932	

NAME	COACHED AT	YEARS	YEAR ELECTED TO HALL OF FAME
	College of Pacific	1922-1946	1951
Vincent Stevenson	Pennsylvania	1903-05	1968
John B. (Jock) Sutherland	Lafayette	1919-1923	
	Pittsburgh	1924-1938	1951
Frank W. Thomas	Chattanooga	1925-1928	
	Alabama	1931-1946	1951
W. Wallace Wade	Alabama	1922-1930	
	Duke	1931-1941	1955
Lynn O. (Pappy) Waldorf	Syracuse	1925	
	Oklahoma City U.	1926-1927	
	Kansas	1928	
	Oklahoma A & M	1929-1933	
	Kansas State	1934	
	Northwestern U.	1935-1946	
	Univ. of California	1947-1951	1966
Glenn S. (Pop) Warner	Georgia	1895-1896	
	Cornell	1897-1898	
	Carlisle	1899-1914	
	Pittsburgh	1915-1924	
	Stanford	1925-1932	
	Temple	1933-1938	1951
E. E. (Tad) Wieman	Michigan	1927-1928	
	Princeton	1938-1942	1956
John W. Wilce	Ohio State	1913-1928	1954
Henry L. Williams	Minnesota	1900-1921	1951
George W. Woodruff	Lehigh	1891	
	Pennsylvania	1892-1901	1963
Fielding H. Yost	Michigan	1900-1926	1951
Robert Zuppke	Illinois	1913-1941	1951